RUBS

OVER 150 RECIPES FOR THE PERFECT SAUCES, MARINADES, SEASONINGS, BASTES, BUTTERS, AND GLAZES

Rubs

13-Digit ISBN: 978-1604337709

10-Digit ISBN: 1604337702

This book may be ordered by mail from the publisher. Please include $5.99 for postage and handling. Please support your local bookseller first!

Books published by Cider Mill Press Book Publishers are available at special discounts for bulk purchases in the United States by corporations, institutions, and other organizations. For more information, please contact the publisher.

Cider Mill Press Book Publishers
"Where good books are ready for press"
PO Box 454
12 Spring Street
Kennebunkport, Maine 04046

Visit us online!
cidermillpress.com

Typography: Avenir, Helvetica Rounded, MinionPro, Neutraface 2, Open Sans, Sentinel, Textured 2
Image Credits: All images used under license from Shutterstock.com.

Printed in China

4 5 6 7 8 9 0

RUBS

OVER 150 RECIPES FOR THE PERFECT SAUCES, MARINADES, SEASONINGS, BASTES, BUTTERS, AND GLAZES

JOHN WHALEN III

CIDER MILL PRESS

BOOK PUBLISHERS

KENNEBUNKPORT, MAINE

Contents

Introduction

Home cooks and seasoned chefs alike know that fresh, natural ingredients are the key to great cuisine. Once you spend the time to find locally sourced meat, why marinate those farm-raised ribs in a pre-packaged sauce? And if you spend the money on organic greens, why dress your nature-fresh salad in a bottled dressing? Making your own rubs, sauces, and marinades is easier than you might think, and these tantalizing recipes will never let you down. These made-from-scratch seasonings are the building blocks to big, bold flavor, and the dozens of homemade recipes in this definitive cookbook will take every dish—from side dishes to meat entrees—to the next level. Pump up your poultry with a unique toasted fennel seed rub, or spice up your beef with a smoked Southern barbecue sauce. You'll love the results!

Rubs

Cooking with rubs requires attention on both the cooking process itself and also the end result. Odds are that if you're going to be grilling over a high-temp, wood-fired flame, you'll want that rub that'll have its flavor crusted and seared onto the exterior of the meat. And on the other hand, if you're using a cast-iron Dutch oven or a slow-cooker, you'll want a rub that'll hug the meat's exterior while seeping into the meat's body and fats. Whether it adds a unique texture, a crisp char, a quick *blast!* of heat, or maybe simply stresses different flavors that were already there, a rub is the best way to spice things up and make a recipe your own.

From the many summers I've spent hanging around the fire-pit, there are a couple small things that I've learned about working with rubs. In the beginning, the first and most important aspect to learning rubs is that you never want to start experimenting with too much rub; you can always add more, but it's impossible to take it back. Along the same lines, you never want to use too nice of a cut of meat as you learn just how much rub you'll want to taste.

When I first started experimenting with different rubs, I often tested rubs on London broils and whole chickens, meats that are inexpensive and offer a large surface space to work with. You'll always want to keep the surface space in mind; if you're looking to prepare a Steak au Poivre, you're going to want to use a Filet Mignon rather than use a London broil... that is, unless you love pepper (I know I do)! You are also likely to find that rubs are used to really enhance a flavor, to capture the overall mood that you're cooking for. Sometimes, in fact, you'll probably find that you'd rather the meat stand on its own with maybe an herbal sauce such as a chimichurri.

Be prepared to experiment with your rubs; find the flavors that you love and run with them. Mix this with that, here and there, learning along the way which flavors are instant classics and which are good for certain occasions. Before anything, make sure that you have a nice bottle of extra-virgin olive oil by your side as you'll want to apply a very thin layer to the meat before adding on the rub.

Southwestern Dry Rub

WORKS BEST WITH: ☑ RED MEAT   ☑ PORK   ☑ POULTRY   ☐ SEAFOOD

FLAVOR: ☑ SPICY   ☐ SWEET   ☐ TANGY   ☑ SAVORY   ☑ SALTY

Using a spoon, combine all of the ingredients in a small bowl and mix thoroughly. Apply to meat when finished.

VARIATION 1: For more heat, add 1 teaspoon of finely chopped habanero pepper! Be sure, however, to have plenty of bread and milk nearby when eating!

VARIATION 2: For a smokier flavor, consider adding 1 or 2 teaspoons of liquid smoke to the ingredients. I recommend Colgin's.

INGREDIENTS

2 teaspoons chili powder

2 teaspoons paprika

1 teaspoon cayenne

1 teaspoon cumin

1 teaspoon ground coriander

1 teaspoon garlic, finely chopped

1 teaspoon kosher salt

1 teaspoon ground black pepper

Rustic Pepper Dry Rub

Using a spoon, combine all of the ingredients in a small bowl and mix thoroughly. Apply to meat when finished.

INGREDIENTS

2 garlic cloves, minced

2 teaspoons thyme, finely chopped

2 teaspoons fresh sea salt

1½ teaspoons coarsely ground black pepper

1½ teaspoons coarsely ground white pepper

1 teaspoon coarsely ground red pepper

1 teaspoon sweet paprika

½ teaspoon onion powder

St. Louis Rub

INGREDIENTS

¼ cup paprika

3 tablespoons garlic powder

2 tablespoons ground black pepper

2 tablespoons kosher salt

2 tablespoons onion powder

1 tablespoon dark brown sugar

1 tablespoon ginger powder

1 tablespoon mustard powder

1 teaspoon celery salt

Using a spoon, combine all of the ingredients in a small bowl and mix thoroughly. Apply to meat when finished.

VARIATION: For a smokier flavor, consider adding 1 or 2 teaspoons of liquid smoke to the ingredients. I recommend Colgin's.

Your Go-To Steak Rub

WORKS BEST WITH: ☑ RED MEAT ☑ PORK ☐ POULTRY ☐ SEAFOOD

FLAVOR: ☐ SPICY ☐ SWEET ☐ TANGY ☑ SAVORY ☐ SALTY

INGREDIENTS

2 tablespoons ground black pepper

2 tablespoons sweet paprika

3 teaspoons kosher salt

1 tablespoon onion powder

1 tablespoon garlic powder

2 teaspoons ground cumin

Using a spoon, combine all of the ingredients in a small bowl and mix thoroughly. Apply to meat when finished.

Smoked Paprika Rub

WORKS BEST WITH: ☑ RED MEAT ☑ PORK ☑ POULTRY ☐ SEAFOOD

FLAVOR: ☐ SPICY ☑ SWEET ☐ TANGY ☑ SAVORY ☐ SALTY

In a small bowl, thoroughly combine all the ingredients and store at room temperature for up to 1 month.

INGREDIENTS

2 tablespoons
smoked paprika

2 teaspoons
ground coriander

2 teaspoons
ground cumin

1 teaspoon
cayenne pepper

1 tablespoon coarsely
ground black pepper

1 tablespoon
fresh sea salt

Classic Seafood Rub

INGREDIENTS

2 tablespoons sweet paprika

2 tablespoons garlic powder

1 tablespoon dry mustard

1 tablespoon ancho chile powder

1 tablespoon onion powder

1 tablespoon coarsely ground black pepper

1 tablespoon fresh sea salt

1 teaspoon ground cinnamon

1 teaspoon ground cumin

In a small bowl, thoroughly combine all the ingredients and store in an airtight container at room temperature for up to 1 month.

Ancho Chile Rub

WORKS BEST WITH: ☑ RED MEAT   ☑ PORK   ☑ POULTRY   ☐ SEAFOOD

FLAVOR: ☑ SPICY   ☐ SWEET   ☐ TANGY   ☑ SAVORY   ☐ SALTY

In a small bowl, mix together all the ingredients and store at room temperature for up to 1 month.

ALTHOUGH YOU MAY THINK THAT THIS IS A VERY HOT RUB, IT IS ACTUALLY FAIRLY MILD. UNLIKE REGULAR CHILE POWDER, ANCHO CHILE POWDER COMES FROM THE ANCHO CHILE PEPPER, WHICH IS ACTUALLY FAIRLY SWEET. AS SUCH, I PAIRED THE SWEET FLAVORS FROM THE ANCHO CHILE WITH THE SWEET FLAVOR FROM THE PAPRIKA.

INGREDIENTS

2 tablespoons sweet paprika

1 tablespoon ancho chile powder

1 tablespoon ground coriander

1 tablespoon ground cumin

2 teaspoons dried oregano

1 tablespoon ground allspice

1 teaspoon onion powder

½ teaspoon cinnamon

Cajun Rub

WORKS BEST WITH: ☑ RED MEAT ☑ PORK ☑ POULTRY ☑ SEAFOOD

FLAVOR: ☐ SPICY ☐ SWEET ☐ TANGY ☑ SAVORY ☑ SALTY

INGREDIENTS

¼ cup sea salt

2 tablespoons ground black pepper

2 teaspoons paprika

2 teaspoons garlic powder

1 teaspoon onion powder

1 teaspoon cayenne pepper

1 teaspoon dried thyme

Using a spoon, combine all of the ingredients in a small bowl and mix thoroughly. Apply to meat when finished.

VARIATION: For a smokier flavor, consider adding 1 or 2 teaspoons of liquid smoke to the ingredients. I recommend Colgin's.

Herbal Rub

WORKS BEST WITH: ☑ RED MEAT ☐ PORK ☑ POULTRY ☑ SEAFOOD

FLAVOR: ☐ SPICY ☐ SWEET ☐ TANGY ☑ SAVORY ☑ SALTY

INGREDIENTS

¼ cup fresh flat-leaf parsley, finely chopped

¼ cup fresh rosemary, finely chopped

4 to 6 medium garlic cloves, diced

1 tablespoon coarsely ground black pepper

2 tablespoons fresh sea salt

¼ cup extra-virgin olive oil

1 In a small bowl, thoroughly combine the parsley, rosemary, garlic, black pepper, and sea salt.

2 Slowly whisk in ¼ cup of olive oil until ingredients form into a smooth paste.

3 Let the rub stand at room temperature for 30 minutes before applying to the meat.

VARIATION: If you would like to turn this into a marinade for a rib roast or other large piece of red meat, increase the amount of extra-virgin olive oil to 1¼ cups. Transfer the marinade into a large bowl, followed by the rib roast. Note, the rib roast will not be completely submerged in the marinade, so be sure to constantly rearrange the rib roast so that all sides are receiving equal marinating times. Let the rib roast marinate for 1 hour.

> WHEN I THINK OF THE PICTURESQUE PRIME RIB, I ALWAYS COME BACK TO A SLOW-ROASTED RIB ROAST ON CHRISTMAS MORNING WITH ROSEMARY AND THYME TIED BETWEEN THE RIBS. ADD EXTRA SEASONING ALL AROUND THE ENDS.

30 Rubs

Coffee Rub

Using a spoon, combine all of the ingredients in a small bowl and mix thoroughly. Apply to meat when finished.

INGREDIENTS

¼ cup ground coffee

2 tablespoons dark brown sugar

2 tablespoons cayenne pepper

2 tablespoons garlic powder

2 tablespoons paprika

2 tablespoons onion powder

1 tablespoon ground cumin

1 tablespoon kosher salt

Indian Curry Rub

WORKS BEST WITH: ☐ RED MEAT ☐ PORK ☑ POULTRY ☑ SEAFOOD

FLAVOR: ☑ SPICY ☐ SWEET ☐ TANGY ☐ SAVORY ☐ SALTY

INGREDIENTS

2 tablespoons yellow
curry powder

1 tablespoon
smoked paprika

1 tablespoon
ground ginger

2 teaspoons
ground cumin

2 teaspoons
ground allspice

2 teaspoons coarsely
ground black pepper

1 teaspoon
fresh sea salt

In a small bowl, thoroughly combine all the ingredients for the rub and store in an airtight container at room temperature for up to 1 month.

Smoked Seafood Dry Rub

WORKS BEST WITH:	☐ RED MEAT	☐ PORK	☑ POULTRY	☑ SEAFOOD
FLAVOR:	☑ SPICY	☐ SWEET	☐ TANGY	☑ SAVORY	☑ SALTY

Using a spoon, combine all of the ingredients in a small bowl and mix thoroughly. Apply to meat when finished.

INGREDIENTS

1 tablespoon paprika

1 tablespoon ground black pepper

1 teaspoon dried basil

1 teaspoon dried tarragon

1 teaspoon garlic, minced

1 teaspoon lemon zest

½ teaspoon chili powder

½ teaspoon onion powder

36 Rubs

Hot and Spicy Chile Rub

WORKS BEST WITH: ☑ RED MEAT ☑ PORK ☑ POULTRY ☑ SEAFOOD

FLAVOR: ☑ SPICY ☐ SWEET ☑ TANGY ☐ SAVORY ☐ SALTY

In a small bowl, thoroughly combine all the ingredients for the rub and store in an airtight container at room temperature for up to 1 month.

INGREDIENTS

3 tablespoons chile powder

3 tablespoons smoked paprika

1 tablespoon dried oregano

2 teaspoons ground cumin

2 teaspoons coarsely ground black pepper

2 teaspoons fresh sea salt

1 teaspoon dried thyme

Dill and Coriander Rub

WORKS BEST WITH: ☐ RED MEAT ☑ PORK ☑ POULTRY ☐ SEAFOOD

FLAVOR: ☐ SPICY ☐ SWEET ☐ TANGY ☑ SAVORY ☑ SALTY

INGREDIENTS

3 tablespoons coarsely ground black pepper

3 tablespoons coriander seeds

2 tablespoons fresh dill, minced

2 medium garlic cloves, minced

2 tablespoons fresh sea salt

1 Combine all of the ingredients in a medium bowl and whisk together thoroughly.

2 Allow the meat to rest at room temperature for 1 hour before seasoning with the rub.

VARIATION: Dill and Coriander Rub can be transformed into a basting marinade for poultry. Just add 1 cup of extra-virgin olive oil to the rub ingredients.

Oregano-Garlic Rub

WORKS BEST WITH: ☑ RED MEAT ☑ PORK ☑ POULTRY ☑ SEAFOOD

FLAVOR: ☐ SPICY ☐ SWEET ☐ TANGY ☑ SAVORY ☑ SALTY

In a small bowl, thoroughly combine all the ingredients for the rub and store in an airtight container at room temperature for up to 1 week.

> FRESH IS BEST. THE FLAVOR OF THE FRESH OREGANO LESSENS AS IT IS STORED FOR LONGER PERIODS OF TIME.

INGREDIENTS

1 tablespoon fresh oregano, finely chopped

2 garlic cloves, minced

2 sprigs thyme, leaves removed

2 teaspoons coarsely ground black pepper

1 teaspoon fresh sea salt

1 teaspoon ground cumin

1 teaspoon ground coriander

Toasted Fennel Seed Rub

WORKS BEST WITH:	☐ RED MEAT	☐ PORK	☑ POULTRY	☑ SEAFOOD
FLAVOR:	☐ SPICY	☐ SWEET	☐ TANGY	☑ SAVORY ☑ SALTY

1 Place a small frying pan over medium heat and toast the fennel and coriander seeds, about 1 to 2 minutes. Remove from heat and let cool.

2 When cool, place the seeds in a small, sealable plastic bag. Using the dull side of the knife, press and grind both the fennel and coriander seeds, as well as the whole black peppercorns, into a rub, and then stir in the fresh sea salt.

INGREDIENTS

¼ cup fennel seeds

1 tablespoon coriander seeds

2 teaspoons whole black peppercorns

2 teaspoons fresh sea salt

Mediterranean Rub

WORKS BEST WITH: ☑ RED MEAT ☑ PORK ☑ POULTRY ☑ SEAFOOD

FLAVOR: ☐ SPICY ☐ SWEET ☐ TANGY ☑ SAVORY ☐ SALTY

INGREDIENTS

2 garlic cloves,
finely chopped

2 tablespoons
rosemary, minced

1 tablespoon
thyme, chopped

1 tablespoon ground
black pepper

2 teaspoons sea salt

1 teaspoon lemon zest

Using a spoon, combine all of the ingredients in a small bowl and mix thoroughly. Apply to meat when finished.

Horseradish Crust

INGREDIENTS

1 stick unsalted butter, softened

6 garlic cloves

¾ cup freshly grated horseradish

¼ cup thyme, finely chopped

2 tablespoons rosemary, minced

3 tablespoons coarsely ground black pepper

2 tablespoons fresh sea salt

1 In a small food processor, pulse together the softened butter, garlic, and horseradish. Transfer to a medium bowl.

2 Mash the remaining ingredients into the bowl and then let stand at room temperate for 30 minutes before applying to the meat.

VARIATION: If you would like to use an oil-based crust, substitute the 1 stick of unsalted butter with ³/₄ cup extra-virgin olive oil. There is now no need for a food processor, so combine all of the ingredients in a medium bowl.

THIS FLAVORFUL RUB COMPLEMENTS A CLASSIC PRIME RIB ROAST. BEFORE TRANSFERRING THE RIB ROAST TO THE OVEN, THE HORSERADISH CRUST SHOULD BE GENEROUSLY APPLIED ON ALL SIDES OF THE MEAT AND MASSAGED IN SO THAT THE FLAVORS OF THE HORSERADISH AND HERBS SEEP INTO THE MARBLED EDGES OF THE RIB ROAST.

Pastrami Rub

WORKS BEST WITH: ☑ RED MEAT ☑ PORK ☐ POULTRY ☐ SEAFOOD

FLAVOR: ☐ SPICY ☐ SWEET ☐ TANGY ☐ SAVORY ☑ SALTY

Using a spoon, combine all of the ingredients in a small bowl and mix thoroughly. Apply to meat when finished.

INGREDIENTS

2 tablespoons coriander powder

4 tablespoons ground black pepper

1 tablespoon mustard powder

2 tablespoons sea salt

2 teaspoons garlic powder

2 teaspoons onion powder

1 tablespoon dark brown sugar

2 tablespoons paprika

Chinese Five-Spice Rub

Using a spoon, combine all of the ingredients in a small bowl and mix thoroughly. Apply to meat when finished.

VARIATION 1: For more of a kick, try adding half of a finely chopped habanero pepper. Be careful, though, the more seeds you include the hotter it will become!

INGREDIENTS

1 tablespoon ground star anise

1 tablespoon ground cinnamon

1 tablespoon ground Sichuan peppercorn

1 tablespoon ground fennel seeds

1 tablespoon ground cloves

1 tablespoon garlic powder

1 tablespoon ground ginger

1 tablespoon sea salt

Barbecued Shrimp Dry Rub

WORKS BEST WITH:	☐ RED MEAT	☐ PORK	☑ POULTRY	☑ SEAFOOD
FLAVOR:	☐ SPICY	☐ SWEET	☐ TANGY	☑ SAVORY ☑ SALTY

INGREDIENTS

1 tablespoon paprika

1 tablespoon ancho chile powder

1 teaspoon garlic powder

1 tablespoon ground black pepper

1 tablespoon sea salt

1 teaspoon dried oregano

1 teaspoon red pepper flakes

Using a spoon, combine all of the ingredients in a small bowl and mix thoroughly. Apply to meat when finished.

Cooking with Rubs

Smoked Spiced

MAKES 4 TO 6 SERVINGS • ACTIVE TIME: 30 MINUTES • TOTAL TIME: 3 HOURS

A seasoned rub puts a different twist on "hot wings."
Serve with celery.

Chicken Wings

1 Place the chicken wings on a roasting pan and put it in the refrigerator. Let rest for at least 2 hours so that the skin on the wings tightens, promoting a crisp wing.

2 One hour before grilling, add the woodchips into a bowl of water and let soak.

3 A half hour before grilling, prepare your gas or charcoal grill to high heat.

4 While the grill heats, remove the wings from the refrigerator and add to a large bowl. Toss with the 2 tablespoons of olive oil.

5 In a medium bowl, combine all of the remaining ingredients.

6 Add the seasoning into the large bowl of chicken wings and toss evenly, making sure that each wing has an equal amount of seasoning.

7 When the grill is ready, at about 450 degrees with the coals lightly covered with ash, scatter the woodchips over the coals and then place the chicken wings on the grill with a good amount of space between them. Cover the grill and cook for about 2 to 3 minutes on each side. Remove from grill when the skin is crispy. Serve immediately.

TOOLS

2 to 3 cups hickory or oak woodchips

INGREDIENTS

2 pounds chicken wings, split

2 tablespoons olive oil

½ small lime, juiced

3 garlic cloves, finely chopped

2 tablespoons flat-leaf parsley, finely chopped

1 tablespoon ground cumin

2 teaspoons paprika

1 teaspoon ground cinnamon

1 teaspoon turmeric

1 teaspoon red pepper flakes

½ teaspoon onion powder

Coarsely ground black pepper

Fresh sea salt

Spicy Shrimp

MAKES 4 TO 6 SERVINGS • ACTIVE TIME: 15 MINUTES • TOTAL TIME: 35 MINUTES

This fiery dish is one of my father's recipes—a summertime favorite. Be sure to have plenty of water and napkins on hand.

INGREDIENTS

1 tablespoon celery salt

¼ teaspoon cayenne pepper

¼ teaspoon paprika

¼ teaspoon ground allspice

1 teaspoon coarsely ground black pepper

½ teaspoon kosher salt

30 large shrimp, peeled and deveined

2 tablespoons olive oil

1 Combine all the spices into a small bowl and mix well.

2 Place the peeled and deveined shrimp to a large bowl and toss with olive oil. Add the spices into the bowl and coat evenly. Set aside while preparing the grill.

3 Preheat your gas or charcoal grill to medium-high heat.

4 When the grill is ready, at about 450 to 500 degrees with the coals lightly covered with ash, add the shrimp to the grill and grill over direct heat. Cook until the shrimp are slightly firm and opaque throughout. Remove from grill and let cool for 5 minutes. Serve warm.

Steak au Poivre

MAKES 2 TO 3 SERVINGS • ACTIVE TIME: 25 MINUTES
TOTAL TIME: 1 HOUR AND 15 MINUTES

This is a classic style that is often paired with a T-bone or porterhouse. However, because of its rich flavor and powerful spice, I recommend applying it to the New York strip or filet mignon. If doing the filet, please follow the recipe on page 69, using the cast-iron skillet and following the given cooking times.

1 Rub both sides of the steaks with olive oil and let rest at room temperature for about 1 hour.

2 A half hour before cooking, prepare your gas or charcoal grill to medium-high heat.

3 Seal the peppercorns in a small, sealable plastic bag and crush with the bottom of a cast-iron skillet.

4 When the grill is ready, at about 400 to 450 degrees with the coals lightly covered with ash, press the peppercorns and sea salt firmly into both sides of the steak. Place the seasoned sides of the steaks on the grill at medium heat and cook for 4 to 5 minutes until they are slightly charred. Turn the steaks and grill for another 3 to 4 minutes for medium-rare, and 4 to 5 minutes for medium. The steaks should feel slightly firm if poked in the center.

5 Remove the steaks from the grill and transfer to a large cutting board. Let rest for 10 minutes, allowing the steaks to properly store their juices and flavor.

6 While the steaks rest, heat the clarified butter in a small saucepan over medium heat. Add the minced shallot, stirring occasionally until softened, about 1 to 2 minutes.

7 Carefully add the Cognac, and if it flames, shake the pan and wait for the flame to burn out. Boil until it has reduced by half.

8 Mix in the coconut milk until the sauce has slightly thickened, about 2 to 3 minutes, and then add the parsley and salt.

9 Place the steaks onto warmed plates and spoon the sauce on top of the steaks.

STEAK INGREDIENTS

2 New York strip steaks, about 1½ inches thick

2 tablespoons olive oil

6 tablespoons black peppercorns

Fresh sea salt

SAUCE INGREDIENTS

3 tablespoons clarified butter

1 shallot, minced

½ cup Cognac

½ cup coconut milk

2 tablespoons fresh parsley, finely chopped

Fresh sea salt

New York Strip

MAKES 2 TO 3 SERVINGS • ACTIVE TIME: 15 MINUTES
TOTAL TIME: 1 HOUR AND 30 MINUTES

For my family, this is our go-to steak. Grilling the New York strip can be fast or slow, depending on your timing. Letting the steak rest at room temperature for an hour is not necessary, so if you are in a rush please feel free to skip it. However, if you do have the time, definitely let the steaks absorb the oil so that the steaks are grizzled and tender when pulled from the grill.

with the olive oil and let rest at room temperature for 1 hour.

2 A half hour before cooking, prepare your gas or charcoal grill to medium-high heat.

3 When the grill is ready, about 400 to 450 degrees with the coals lightly covered with ash, season one side of the steaks with half of the coarsely ground pepper and sea salt.

4 Place the seasoned sides of the steaks on the grill at medium heat. Wait 3 to 5 minutes until they are slightly charred. One minute before flipping, season the uncooked sides of the steaks with the remaining pepper and sea salt. Turn the steaks and grill for another 3 to 4 minutes for medium-rare, and 4 to 5 minutes for medium. The steaks should feel slightly firm if poked in the center.

5 Remove the steaks from the grill and transfer to a large cutting board. Let stand for 10 minutes, allowing the steaks to properly store their juices and flavor. Serve warm, and if desired, garnish with a little rosemary.

2 New York strip steaks about 1½ inches thick

2 tablespoons olive oil

Coarsely ground black pepper

Fresh sea salt

Rosemary for garnish if desired

TIP: FOR MORE OF A NATURAL FLAVOR, LIGHT A FIRE USING DRY LOGS AND BURN DOWN TO COALS. THIS WILL TAKE THE GRILL ABOUT 45 MINUTES TO PREHEAT, AND THE STEAKS WILL NEED TO COOK FOR ABOUT ONE MINUTE LONGER THAN DESIRED TEMPERATURE ON EACH SIDE.

Porterhouse

MAKES 2 TO 3 SERVINGS • ACTIVE TIME: 20 MINUTES
TOTAL TIME: 1 HOUR AND 45 MINUTES

This is by far one of the most filling and flavorful steaks available—it boasts half New York strip and half filet mignon. Ask your butcher to keep a large part of the filet mignon intact (they sometimes trim it too much).

1 Rub both sides of the steaks with olive oil and let rest at room temperature for about 1 hour.

2 A half hour before cooking, prepare your gas or charcoal grill to medium-high heat.

3 When the grill is ready, about 400 to 450 degrees with the coals lightly covered with ash, season one side of the steaks with half of the coarsely ground pepper and sea salt. Place the seasoned sides of the steaks on the grill and cook for about 5 to 6 minutes, seasoning the tops of the steaks while waiting.

4 When the steaks are charred, flip and cook for 4 to 5 more minutes for medium-rare, and 6 to 7 for medium. The steaks should feel slightly firm if poked in the center.

5 Remove the steaks from the grill and transfer to a large cutting board. Let stand for 10 minutes, allowing the steaks to properly store their juices and flavor. Serve warm.

INGREDIENTS

2 porterhouse steaks, about 1½ inches thick

4 tablespoons olive oil

Coarsely ground black pepper

Fresh sea salt

TIP: FOR A BIT OF A SAN FRANCISCO FLARE, MIX THE OLIVE OIL WITH A COUPLE TEASPOONS OF FINELY CHOPPED GARLIC BEFORE MARINATING THE STEAKS.

Filet Mignon

**MAKES 2 TO 3 SERVINGS • ACTIVE TIME: 20 MINUTES
TOTAL TIME: 1 HOUR AND 30 MINUTES**

The filet is one of the harder steaks to grill due to its 2-inch thickness and relatively small surface area, proving it difficult to remain upright on the grate. As such, I recommend using a seasoned cast-iron skillet over the grill for the initial searing and then transferring the filets to the oven.

1 Tie the butcher's string tightly around each steak. Then rub both sides of the steaks with 2 tablespoons of the olive oil and let rest at room temperature for about 1 hour.

2 A half hour before cooking, place the cast-iron skillet on the grate and prepare your gas or charcoal grill to medium-high heat. Leave the grill covered while heating, as it will add a faint smoky flavor to the skillet.

3 When the coals are ready, about 400 degrees with the coals lightly covered with ash, season one side of the steaks with half of the coarsely ground pepper and sea salt.

4 Spread the remaining tablespoon of olive oil in the skillet, and then place the steaks, seasoned sides down, into the cast-iron skillet. Wait 2 to 3 minutes until they are slightly charred, seasoning the uncooked sides of the steaks with the remaining pepper and sea salt while waiting. Flip the steaks and sear for another 2 to 3 minutes. Remove from the skillet and let rest, uncovered, for 30 minutes.

5 Preheat the oven to 400 degrees.

6 Put the steaks back into the cast-iron skillet and place in the oven. For medium-rare, cook for 11 to 13 minutes, and for medium, cook for 14 to 15.

7 Remove the steaks from the oven and transfer to a large cutting board. Let stand for 10 minutes. Detach the butcher's string from the steaks and serve warm.

TOOLS

Butcher's twine

Cast-iron skillet

INGREDIENTS

2 filet mignon steaks, about 2 to 2½ inches thick

3 tablespoons olive oil

Coarsely ground black pepper

Fresh sea salt

TIP: WHEN YOU REMOVE THE STEAKS FROM THE GRILL, DO NOT RELINQUISH THE FIRE, AS IT COULD STILL BE USED TO GRILL CUBANELLE OR SHISHITO PEPPERS.

Flank Steak

MAKES 2 SERVINGS • ACTIVE TIME: 15 MINUTES
TOTAL TIME: 1 HOUR AND 15 MINUTES

The flank steak, often hailed as a chewy cut of meat, is one of the hardest to cook properly. Stay close to the grill after you put the steaks on as it is very easy for them to be overcooked. Also, because the steak is very thin, be sure to prepare the grill to medium-high heat so that the edges will be charred and crisp.

1 Rub the steak with a mixture of the olive oil, rosemary, and thyme. Let rest at room temperature for 1 hour.

2 A half hour before cooking, prepare your gas or charcoal grill to medium-high heat.

3 When the grill is ready, about 400 to 450 degrees with the coals lightly covered with ash, season one side of the steak with half of the coarsely ground pepper and sea salt. Place the seasoned side of the steak on the grill and cook for about 4 to 5 minutes, seasoning the uncooked side of the steak while waiting. When the steak seems charred, gently flip and cook for 4 to 5 more minutes for medium-rare and 6 more minutes for medium. The steak should feel slightly firm if poked in the center.

4 Remove the steak from the grill and transfer to a large cutting board. Let stand for 6 to 8 minutes. Slice the steak diagonally into long, thin slices. Serve warm.

INGREDIENTS

1 flank steak
about 1 to 1½ pounds

2 tablespoons olive oil

2 sprigs rosemary,
leaves removed

2 sprigs thyme,
leaves removed

Coarsely ground
black pepper

Fresh sea salt

TIP: DUE TO THE FLANK'S TOUGHNESS, IT IS ESSENTIAL TO SLICE THIS STEAK INTO VERY THIN STRIPS.

Chipotle Rib Eye

For big flavor, grill a couple of Chipotle rib eyes and serve with red wine.

1 Combine the rub ingredients and mix thoroughly.

2 Rub a very thin layer of olive oil to both sides of the steaks and then generously apply the dry rub, firmly pressing it all around the steak. Let rest at room temperature for at least 1 hour.

3 A half hour before cooking, prepare your gas or charcoal grill to medium-high heat.

4 When the grill is ready, at about 400 to 450 degrees with the coals lightly covered with ash, place the steaks on the grill and cook for about 6 to 7 minutes until blood begins to rise from the tops. When the steaks are charred, flip and cook for 4 to 5 more minutes for medium-rare or 5 to 6 more minutes for medium. The steaks should feel slightly firm if poked in the center.

5 Remove the steaks from the grill and transfer to a large cutting board. Let stand for 5 to 10 minutes, allowing the steaks to properly store their juices and flavor. Serve warm.

RUB INGREDIENTS

2 dry chipotle peppers, seeded and finely minced

1 tablespoon dried oregano

1 tablespoon dried cilantro

1 tablespoon coarsely ground black pepper

2 teaspoons ground cumin

1 teaspoon onion powder

½ teaspoon dry mustard

Fresh sea salt

STEAK INGREDIENTS

2 bone-in rib eyes, about 1¼ to 1½ inches thick

1 tablespoon olive oil

Chile-Rubbed London Broil

MAKES 2 TO 3 SERVINGS • ACTIVE TIME: 30 MINUTES
TOTAL TIME: 1 HOUR AND 30 MINUTES

The London broil is an economical steak for large family gatherings. Start with a tasty rub, and finish by slicing the London broil diagonally into thin strips.

1 Combine the rub ingredients and mix thoroughly. Set aside.

2 Rub a very thin layer of olive oil to both sides of the steaks and then generously apply the dry rub, firmly pressing it all around the steak. Let rest at room temperature for at least 1 hour.

3 A half hour before cooking, prepare your gas or charcoal grill to medium-high heat.

4 When the grill is ready, at about 400 to 450 degrees with the coals lightly covered with ash, place the steaks on the grill. Cook until blood begins to rise from the tops, about 4 to 5 minutes. When the steaks are charred, flip and cook for another 3 to 4 minutes for medium-rare or 5 to 6 more minutes for medium.

5 Remove the steak from the grill and transfer to a large cutting board. Let stand for 6 to 8 minutes. Slice the steak diagonally into long, thin slices. Serve warm.

RUB INGREDIENTS

1 cup ancho chile powder

2 tablespoons paprika

1 tablespoon coarsely ground black pepper

1 tablespoon sea salt

2 teaspoons ground cumin

1 teaspoon cayenne pepper

1 teaspoon dry mustard

1 teaspoon dried oregano

STEAK INGREDIENTS

1 London broil steak, about ¾ to 1 inch thick

1 to 2 tablespoons olive oil

TIP: DUE TO THE LONDON BROIL'S TOUGHNESS, IT IS ESSENTIAL TO SLICE THIS STEAK INTO VERY THIN STRIPS.

Rotisserie-Grilled

The rotisserie is a great tool on a summer evening for a quick prime rib. One of my favorite elements to this meal is that its timing is extremely easy to wrap your head around: only 16 to 18 minutes per pound. When you rotisserie the meat, the constant, slow turning of the meat ensures it will receive equal amounts of heat, which ultimately quickens the cooking process. Place an aluminum pan underneath the rib roast as it's cooking for the juices that will fall out—they can be used for a classic au jus.

filled with water and let soak. Set alongside the grill.

6 Spit the rib roast with the rotisserie's prongs so that the spit goes through the center of the rib roast toward the bone. As an added precaution, truss the rib roast with butcher's twine around the spit.

Continued on next page >

2 tablespoons coarsely ground black pepper

3 bunches fresh thyme

3 bunches fresh rosemary

< Continued from previous page

7 Set a large aluminum roasting pan on the grill and then place the rib roast on the rotisserie above the pan, so that the juices will fall into the dish (see pages 226 to 229 for au jus guidelines).

8 Cover the grill and roast the prime rib at a low speed for about $2\frac{1}{2}$ hours (16 to 18 minutes per pound, to be more exact). At this point, an instant read thermometer should record the internal heat as below 125 degrees.

9 Heat the smoking box and when hot, throw a handful of woodchips into the heat periodically so that you continuously smoke the prime rib while it finishes roasting—about another 30 minutes, until the thermometer reads 125 degrees.

10 Remove the rib roast from the rotisserie and transfer to a large carving board. Let stand for 10 minutes before carving, allowing the meat to properly store its juices.

Californian Coffee Prime Rib

MAKES 6 TO 8 SERVINGS • **ACTIVE TIME: 1 HOUR** • **TOTAL TIME: 4 HOURS**

A coffee-based rub is nearly always paired with beef because of its bold, though soft flavors. The coffee rub is heavy, but it's very accessible because its flavors largely remain on the outside of the roast. When applied to the rib roast, the flavors will get into the cap of the roast, though for the most part, the finely ground coffee and split peppercorns will form a thick, charred crust on the outside of the roast.

1 Remove the rib roast from the refrigerator 1 hour before cooking and let stand at room temperature.

2 Preheat the oven to 450 degrees.

3 Place the whole black peppercorns in a small, sealable bag and seal tightly. Place the bag on a flat surface and then, using the bottom of a heavy pan such as a cast-iron skillet, firmly pound the peppercorns so that they split into large pieces (ideally, larger than what a traditional pepper mill would do). Remove the split peppercorns from the bag and add to a small bowl. Mix in the fresh sea salt.

4 To the peppercorns and salt, add the coffee, thyme, sugar, mustard, and paprika and combine so it forms an evenly distributed rub.

5 When the meat's temperature has risen, generously apply the extra-virgin olive oil to the prime rib. Using your hands, apply the rub to the prime rib, making sure that all areas of the meat under the fat-cap also receive the rub. If you'd like to add a rosemary element to the prime rib, divide bunches of rosemary evenly and place in between the ribs. Tie firmly with butcher's twine so the rosemary stays in place while roasting.

6 Transfer the coffee-rubbed prime rib to a large rack set in a roasting pan. Then transfer the pan to the oven and sear for about 15 minutes.

Continued on next page >

INGREDIENTS

A 6-rib rib roast

2 tablespoons whole black peppercorns

2 tablespoons fresh sea salt

¼ cup finely ground coffee

3 tablespoons thyme, finely chopped

2 tablespoons dark brown sugar

2 teaspoons ground mustard

1 teaspoon smoked paprika

3 tablespoons extra-virgin olive oil

3 bunches fresh rosemary (optional)

< Continued from previous page

7 Reduce the heat to 325 degrees and cook for $2^1/_2$ to 3 hours, until a thermometer registers 125 degrees for medium-rare. During the roasting process, the crust of the rib roast may begin to brown—if that is the case, gently cover the rib roast with a sheet of aluminum foil in order to help maintain the moisture on the cap of the roast.

8 Remove the rib roast from the oven, transfer to a large carving board, and let stand for about 10 minutes before carving, allowing it to properly store its juices and flavor.

I FIRST HAD THIS STEAK WHEN I WAS SIXTEEN, TRAVELING WITH MY FAMILY TO FLORENCE, ITALY. WE HAD BEEN WALKING THE STREETS FOR NEARLY TWO HOURS LOOKING FOR A PLACE TO EAT. IT WAS 5PM ON NEW YEAR'S EVE AND EVERYTHING WAS BOOKED. FINALLY, WE CAME ACROSS A SMALL STOREFRONT WITH FRESH CUTS OF MEAT HANGING IN THE WINDOW AND A MAN LEANING AGAINST THE DOOR. WE ASKED HIM IF HE HAD ROOM FOR FIVE. HE LOOKED AT HIS WATCH AND ASKED US IF WE COULD EAT IN UNDER 40 MINUTES. WE TOLD HIM WE WOULD AND QUICKLY ORDERED FOUR BISTECCAS ALLA FIORENTINA WITH GRILLED TOMATOES WITH THYME AND OLIVE OIL. THE STEAKS CAME OUT 15 MINUTES LATER, STILL SIZZLING WITH THE OIL SHINING IN THE CANDLELIGHT.

Bistecca alla Fiorentina

MAKES 2 SERVINGS • ACTIVE TIME: 30 MINUTES
TOTAL TIME: 1 HOUR AND 45 MINUTES

Cooked to medium-rare, these steaks will stand by themselves. There is no real need for a side—maybe just a thin slice of lemon—but if you really want one, I suggest grilled tomatoes with garlic.

1 Place the steaks in a roasting pan or bowl. Then, rub the steaks with the rosemary, garlic, and ½ cup of the olive oil, and let rest at room temperature for 1 hour.

2 A half hour before cooking, prepare your gas or charcoal grill to medium-high heat.

3 When the grill is ready, about 400 to 450 degrees with the coals lightly covered with ash, season one side of the steak with half of the coarsely ground pepper and sea salt. Place the seasoned-side of the steak on the grill and cook for 5 minutes, basting the unseasoned sides with the remaining olive oil every 30 seconds. Season the top sides with the remaining salt and pepper and then gently flip and cook for 4 to 6 more minutes, still basting until finished. The steak should feel slightly firm if poked in the center.

4 Remove the steaks from the grill and transfer to a large cutting board. Let stand for 6 to 8 minutes. Serve warm.

INGREDIENTS

2 T-bone steaks, about ¾ to 1¼ inches thick

1 sprig of rosemary, leaves removed

4 cloves garlic, crushed

1 cup olive oil

Coarsely ground black pepper

Fresh sea salt

Blackened Texas Brisket with Coleslaw

**MAKES 3 TO 4 SERVINGS • ACTIVE TIME: 8 TO 9 HOURS
TOTAL TIME: 10 TO 11 HOURS**

Beef brisket is a cut from the chest muscles and is known for its toughness when cooked over high-heat. To tenderize the meat, we must grill the brisket at low-heat, 225 to 250 degrees, for a long period of time, about 5 to 7 hours. When cooked properly, the brisket will be tender and juicy. Coleslaw is the perfect accompaniment.

TOOLS

6 to 8 cups hickory
or oak woodchips

1 large aluminum
foil pan

1 smoker box
(if using a gas grill)

BRISKET
INGREDIENTS

1 center-cut beef
brisket, 5 to 6
pounds and about
½ inches thick

2 tablespoons
olive oil

RUB INGREDIENTS

¼ cup paprika

3 tablespoons
coarsely ground
black pepper

1 tablespoon ground
chipotle chile

1 tablespoon
chili powder

2 teaspoons
cayenne pepper

1 teaspoon
ground cumin

1 teaspoon
dried oregano

Fresh sea salt

COLESLAW
INGREDIENTS

¼ cup apple
cider vinegar

¼ cup raw honey

1 garlic clove, minced

1 teaspoon celery salt

1 teaspoon coarsely
ground black pepper

1 teaspoon
fresh sea salt

½ teaspoon dry mustard

½ head purple cabbage

½ head green cabbage

2 carrots, peeled and
finely chopped

Continued on next page >

< Continued from previous page

1 Combine the rub ingredients in a small bowl and whisk thoroughly. Rub the brisket with the olive oil and then generously apply the rub ingredients, firmly kneading it into the meat. Wrap the brisket in plastic wrap and let rest at room temperature from 2 to 10 hours (the longer the better).

2 While waiting, soak the woodchips in water for 1 to 2 hours.

3 A half hour before cooking, prepare your gas or charcoal grill to low heat: about 250 degrees. You want to designate two separate heat sections on the grill: one for direct heat and the other for indirect heat. To do this, simply arrange the coals toward one side of the grill.

4 When the grill is ready (the coals should be lightly covered with ash), drain 1 cup of the woodchips and spread over the coals or pour in the smoker box. Place the grate on the grill and then lay the brisket, fatty-side up, in the large aluminum pan. Position the pan over the cool section of the grill and then cover with the lid, aligning the air vent away from the woodchips so that their smoke rolls around the brisket before escaping. Cook for 5½ to 6 hours, rekindling the fire with coals and fresh wood chips every hour or so. When the internal temperature reads 190 to 200 degrees and the meat is very tender when pierced with a fork, remove from the grill.

5 Transfer to a large cutting board and let stand for 20 to 30 minutes without touching.

6 While waiting, put a saucepan over medium-low heat and add all the ingredients for the coleslaw except for the cabbage and carrots. Bring to a boil and simmer for 5 minutes. Add the cabbage and carrots to a medium-sized bowl. Remove the dressing from heat and slowly stir into the cabbage and carrots. Refrigerate for 30 minutes.

7 Slice the brisket diagonally into ¼-inch strips and serve with coleslaw.

Rosemary-Lemon

MAKES 4 SERVINGS • ACTIVE TIME: 45 MINUTES • TOTAL TIME: 14 HOURS

As the rosemary and lemon flavors are relatively soft, they go perfectly when used in a marinade for a leg of lamb.

INGREDIENTS

¾ cup olive oil

¼ cup fresh rosemary leaves, coarsely chopped

3 lemons, juiced

4 garlic cloves, finely chopped

A 6-pound boneless leg of lamb, butterflied

Coarsely ground black pepper

Fresh sea salt

1 The day before grilling, combine the olive oil, rosemary leaves, lemon juice, and garlic in a roasting pan and mix thoroughly.

2 Place the leg of lamb on a large carving board. Season generously with coarsely ground black pepper and sea salt, kneading the lamb so that the pepper and salt are pressed in. Place the seasoned leg of lamb in the roasting pan with the marinade.

3 Transfer the pan to the refrigerator and let the meat marinate overnight. Note that the olive oil may not cover the meat entirely; in that case, flip the meat once halfway through the marinating process.

4 An hour before grilling, remove the leg of lamb from the refrigerator and let stand at room temperature for at least 1 hour. Reserve the remaining marinade as it will be used for brushing the meat while it is grilled.

5 A half-hour before grilling, prepare your gas or charcoal grill to medium-high heat.

Leg of Lamb

6 When the coals are ready, at about 400 degrees with the coals lightly covered with ash, place the marinated leg of lamb on the grill and cook for about 16 minutes per side for medium-rare, 17 minutes for medium. While grilling, brush the remaining marinade on top of the lamb. When finished, transfer the lamb to a large carving board and let rest for 15 minutes, allowing for the meat to properly store its juices.

7 Before serving, slice the lamb into $\frac{1}{2}$-inch-thick diagonal strips. Serve warm.

Grill-Roasted Rack of Lamb with Garlic-Herb Crust

MAKES 5 TO 6 SERVINGS • ACTIVE TIME: 20 MINUTES • TOTAL TIME: 14 HOURS

Because rack of lamb is a very delicate meat, be sure to give it the time to marinate overnight. I suggest pairing this with a glass of red wine.

1 The night before grilling, combine the olive oil, garlic, and lemon zest in a large sealable plastic bag. Pat dry the racks of lamb, and then season them with coarsely ground black pepper and fresh sea salt, kneading the pepper and salt deeply into the meaty sections of the lamb. Add the racks of lamb to the plastic bag and place it in the refrigerator. Let marinate overnight.

2 An hour and a half before grilling, remove the racks of lamb from the refrigerator and let rest, uncovered and at room temperature.

3 A half hour before grilling, prepare your gas or charcoal grill to medium heat.

4 While the grill heats, combine all the crust ingredients in a small bowl. Generously apply the crust ingredients to the lamb, being sure to apply most of the crust on the meaty side of the rack.

5 When the grill is ready, at about 400 degrees with the coals lightly covered with ash, place the meaty side of the racks of lamb on the grill and cook for about 3 to 4 minutes. When the crusts are browned, flip the racks of lamb and grill for another 5 minutes for medium-rare.

6 Transfer the racks of lamb from the grill to a large carving board and let rest for about 10 minutes before slicing between the ribs. Serve warm.

LAMB INGREDIENTS

2 tablespoons olive oil

2 garlic cloves, finely chopped

1 teaspoon lemon zest

Two 8-rib racks of lamb, about 1 lb. each

Coarsely ground black pepper

Fresh sea salt

CRUST INGREDIENTS

4 garlic cloves, finely chopped

½ small shallot, finely chopped

¼ cup fresh flat-leaf parsley, coarsely chopped

2 tablespoons fresh rosemary, finely chopped

1 tablespoon fresh thyme, finely chopped

1 tablespoon olive oil

Coarsely ground black pepper

Fresh sea salt

Grill-Roasted Pork Loin

**MAKES 5 TO 6 SERVINGS • ACTIVE TIME: 1 HOUR AND 15 MINUTES
TOTAL TIME: 2 HOURS**

These basic ingredients bring out the natural juices and flavors. Just be sure to use a pan that can go from the oven to the grill.

INGREDIENTS

5 tablespoons olive oil

1 or 2 sprigs fresh rosemary

2¼ pounds loin of pork

Fresh sea salt

Coarsely ground black pepper

1 Fire up your grill and allow the coals to settle into a temperature of approximately 350 degrees. While the grill is heating, slowly sauté the olive oil and rosemary in a cast-iron or All Clad–style high heat–friendly pan. Be sure the pan is oven-and-grill friendly, as you will be placing this pan directly onto your grill.

2 After the oil and rosemary have been thoroughly heated and the flavors of the sprigs are infused throughout the oil (about 10 to 12 minutes), rub your pork loin with sea salt and fresh cracked pepper to your desired seasoning, and place the pork loin into the pan, turning it so the entire loin is covered with the heated oil.

3 Baste for 5 to 10 minutes at a medium heat until the loin begins to brown. Once your grill has reached the desired temperature, move the entire pan to your grill grate.

4 Cover your grill and allow the pork to cook for 45 minutes, turning and basting the pork occasionally so all sides are thoroughly browned from the heat of the hot pan.

5 At about 45 minutes, remove the pork loin from the pan and place directly on the grate. Continue to baste your pork loin using the infused oil from the pan, turning the loin evenly so the entire roast meets the heat side of your grill. Baste and turn for an additional 15 or so minutes or until the roast meets your desired temperature.

6 Remove from fire and let the loin rest for 10 to 12 minutes. Carve and serve with sides of your choice.

> FOR ANY OVEN-TO-GRILL RECIPE, AVOID USING ANY COOKWARE THAT HAS A PLASTIC, WOOD, OR SYNTHETIC-TYPE HANDLE. IT IS BEST IF THE PAN HAS ROUNDED SIDES, HIGH ENOUGH TO PREVENT THE OIL FROM SPILLING OR FLARING UP WHEN BASTING.

Indian Chicken with Mango-Avocado Salad

MAKES 4 TO 5 SERVINGS • ACTIVE TIME: 40 MINUTES • TOTAL TIME: 2 HOURS

Although this dish may look complicated, it is really straightforward and quick.

CHICKEN INGREDIENTS

6 to 8 chicken drumsticks and wings, about 3½ pounds (or chicken thighs, if preferred)

3 to 4 tablespoons olive oil

1 medium yellow onion, finely chopped

2 scallions, finely chopped

½ small lemon or lime, juiced

3 garlic cloves, minced

3 teaspoons garam masala

½ teaspoon dried thyme

1 teaspoon ground turmeric

1 teaspoon cayenne pepper

Coarsely ground black pepper

1 teaspoon fresh sea salt

SALAD INGREDIENTS

2 medium mangos, cubed

2 large avocados, halved, pitted, and cubed

¼ small red onion, coarsely chopped

2 cups chopped tomatoes

1 cup fresh basil leaves, thinly sliced

½ small lemon or lime, juiced

1 tablespoon olive oil

2 teaspoons coarsely ground black pepper

1 teaspoon fresh sea salt

1 Wash and dry the chicken drumsticks and wings and then rub with olive oil. Let rest at room temperature for about 30 minutes.

2 In a small roasting pan, combine the remaining chicken ingredients and spread evenly along the bottom of the pan. Rub the chicken pieces with the Indian spices. Set aside and let rest for about 1 hour.

3 A half hour before grilling, prepare your gas or charcoal grill to medium heat.

4 When the grill is ready, at about 400 degrees with the coals lightly covered with ash, place the drumsticks and wings on the grill and season the tops with the remaining spices. Grill for about 30 minutes, rotating onto each side.

5 While the chicken is cooking, combine the mango, avocado, red onion, cherry tomatoes, and basil and mix well. Next, add the lemon or lime juice and olive oil and mix lightly. Season with pepper and salt and set aside.

6 Remove the drumsticks and wings from the grill when the skins are crispy and charred. Let rest for 5 minutes and then serve alongside the mango-avocado salad.

Smoked Pulled Barbeque Chicken Sandwiches

MAKES 4 TO 6 SERVINGS • ACTIVE TIME: 40 MINUTES • TOTAL TIME: 10 HOURS

To get the perfect "pulled" and "shredded" texture and still achieve the smoked flavor, you must simply grill the chicken first and then quickly braise it in a cast-iron skillet on the grill at medium heat.

TOOLS

2 to 3 cups hickory or oak woodchips

Cast-iron skillet

CHICKEN INGREDIENTS

1 teaspoon chili powder

¼ teaspoon cayenne pepper

2 teaspoons Tabasco

½ teaspoon chipotle chile powder

2 to 3 pounds skinless, boneless chicken breasts

6 hamburger buns

BARBECUE SAUCE INGREDIENTS

2 tablespoons clarified butter

4 garlic cloves, finely chopped

½ cup white onion, minced

½ medium shallot, finely chopped

¾ cup tomatoes, crushed

1 cup apple cider vinegar

2 tablespoons honey

Coarsely ground black pepper

Fresh sea salt

Continued on next page >

< Continued from previous page

1 In a large bowl, mix the chili powder, cayenne pepper, Tabasco, and chile powder, then add the chicken breasts. Rub the spices over the chicken and then place the bowl in the refrigerator. Let marinate for 2 to 12 hours, the longer the better.

2 An hour before grilling, add the woodchips to a bowl of water and let soak. At the same time, prepare your gas or charcoal grill to medium heat. Place a cast-iron skillet on the grill while heating so that it develops a faint smoky flavor.

3 When the grill is ready, at about 350 to 400 degrees with the coals lightly covered with ash, scatter half of the woodchips over the coals and then place the chicken breasts on the grill. Cover the grill, aligning the air vent away from the woodchips so that their smoke rolls around the chicken breasts before escaping. Cook for about 7 to 8 minutes on each side and then remove from grill. Transfer the chicken to a large cutting board, let rest for 5 minutes, and then shred the chicken with a fork in each hand. Set aside.

4 Scatter the remaining woodchips over the coals and add the clarified butter to the skillet. When hot, add the garlic, onion, and shallot and sauté until the garlic is golden and the onion and shallot are translucent. Add the crushed tomatoes, vinegar, honey, pepper, and salt and simmer for about 15 minutes, or until the barbecue sauce has thickened. Mix in the chicken and reduce heat. Cook for 5 more minutes and then remove from heat.

5 Let the chicken rest for 5 minutes to properly absorb the sauce, then serve on warm buns.

Cajun Turkey with

MAKES 8 TO 10 SERVINGS • ACTIVE TIME: 3 HOURS
TOTAL TIME: 10 TO 24 HOURS

This is a great meal when cooking for a large family gathering. Slice the turkey completely after grilling and then set aside the extra meat for turkey and cranberry sandwiches the next day.

CAJUN TURKEY INGREDIENTS

A 12- to 14-pound turkey

8 cups cold water

½ cup kosher salt

2 tablespoons clarified butter

2 tablespoons onion powder

2 tablespoons paprika

1 tablespoon cayenne pepper

1 tablespoon garlic powder

1 tablespoon ground oregano

1 tablespoon dried thyme

1 tablespoon coarsely ground black pepper

1 tablespoon fresh sea salt

CRANBERRY SAUCE INGREDIENTS

4 cups raw cranberries

⅓ cup honey

½ cup orange juice

½ small lemon, juiced

Cranberry Sauce

1 Place the turkey in a large stockpot, and submerge with about 8 cups of water; if you need more, make sure to increase the amount of kosher salt. Let the turkey brine at room temperature for 6 to 12 hours.

2 For the cranberry sauce, combine the cranberries, honey, orange juice, and lemon juice in a medium saucepan over medium heat. Simmer for about 15 minutes, until the sauce thickens and the berries have broken apart. Transfer to a bowl and refrigerate overnight.

3 Remove the turkey and pat dry. In a small bowl, mix together the Cajun spices. Spoon the clarified butter over the turkey and distribute evenly, and then rub the spices all around the turkey. Let rest at room temperature for 1 to 2 hours.

4 Prepare your gas or charcoal grill to medium-low heat and designate two separate heat sections on the grill, one for direct heat and the other for indirect. To do this, simply arrange the coals toward one side of the grill.

5 When the grill is ready, at about 350 to 400 degrees with the coals lightly covered with ash, place the turkey over indirect heating and grill for about 2 to $2\frac{1}{2}$ hours. While grilling, you want to replenish the coals and flip the turkey every 45 minutes. Insert a meat thermometer into the thickest part of the thigh; when finished, the turkey should be at 165 degrees.

6 Remove the turkey from the grill and cover with aluminum foil. Let rest for 45 minutes to 1 hour before carving. Serve alongside cranberry sauce.

Grilled Quail on Citrus Spinach

MAKES 4 SERVINGS • **ACTIVE TIME: 20 MINUTES** • **TOTAL TIME: 2 HOURS**

This is an impressive springtime meal. Lay the quail on top of the spinach salad with pine nuts, and serve with white wine.

Salad with Pine Nuts

1 Coat the quail with olive oil and then season with ground pepper and sea salt. Let stand at room temperature for 1 to 1½ hours.

2 While the quail rest, turn to the salad, adding ½ cup of the olive oil, vinegar, lime and orange juices, and shallots into a small bowl and then seasoning with pepper and salt.

3 In a separate, large bowl, mix the spinach, tomatoes, currants, sunflower seeds, and sesame seeds and set aside.

4 In a small frying pan, heat 1 tablespoon of olive oil and then add the pine nuts. Toast until the pine nuts are brown. Remove from heat and mix into the spinach.

5 Prepare your gas or charcoal grill to medium-high heat.

6 When the grill is ready, at about 400 to 450 degrees with the coals lightly covered with ash, place the quail skin-side up for about 5 minutes until the skin is lightly browned. Flip and grill for 2 more minutes. When finished, transfer quail to a large cutting board and let rest, uncovered, for 5 to 10 minutes.

7 Combine the salad dressing and salad, and then serve with quail.

QUAIL INGREDIENTS

4 to 6 quail, butterflied (see "Chicken Under Brick," page 310)

2 tablespoons olive oil

Coarsely ground black pepper

Fresh sea salt

SALAD INGREDIENTS

½ cup, plus 1 tablespoon olive oil

4 tablespoons white wine vinegar

½ small lime, juiced

¼ orange, juiced

1 small shallot, finely chopped

Coarsely ground black pepper

Fresh sea salt

4 cups baby spinach

½ to 1 cup cherry tomatoes, quartered

4 tablespoons currants

3 tablespoons sunflower seeds

2 tablespoons sesame seeds

½ cup pine nuts

Grilled Salmon and

MAKES 4 SERVINGS • ACTIVE TIME: 25 MINUTES • TOTAL TIME: 50 MINUTES

A classic grilled filet of salmon is a dish that can often stand by itself due to its fresh flavors. This recipe serves the salmon with grilled red bell peppers. If you'd like a second vegetable, steamed green beans or asparagus are good options.

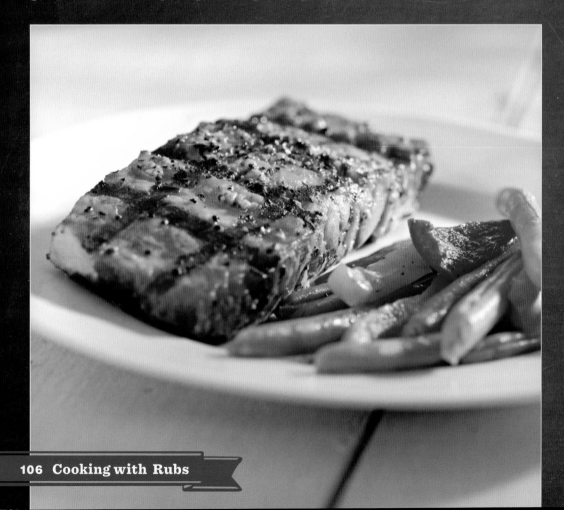

Bell Peppers

1 Place the salmon on a large platter and coat evenly with olive oil, coarsely ground black pepper, and salt. Take the lemon half and, holding it in the palm of your hand, squeeze it gently over the salmon. Let rest at room temperature.

2 A half hour before cooking, place a cast-iron skillet on your gas or charcoal grill and prepare to medium heat. Leave the grill covered while heating, as it will add a faint smoky flavor to the skillet.

3 When the grill is ready, at about 400 degrees with the coals lightly covered with ash, add the bells peppers to the cast-iron skillet and let cook, turning semi-frequently, until the peppers are nearly charred and wrinkled, about 20 minutes. Remove the peppers and let cool.

4 Place the salmon on the grill and cook for about 5 to 6 minutes per side, until the fish is flakey when pierced with a fork. Transfer to a cutting board and let rest for 5 to 10 minutes.

5 Take the peppers and remove the stems and seeds. Next, cut the peppers into long strips and add to a medium bowl. Mix in the olive oil, balsamic vinegar, and thyme and serve by the salmon fillets.

SALMON INGREDIENTS

4 salmon filets, about 4-inch squares

2 tablespoons olive oil

Coarsely ground black pepper

Fresh sea salt

½ lemon

BELL PEPPER INGREDIENTS

4 red bell peppers

2 tablespoons olive oil

1 teaspoon balsamic vinegar

1 sprig thyme, leaves removed

Grilled Whole Striped Bass

When I'm able to catch a striped bass off our little Boston Whaler, I season it with fresh-squeezed orange juice, rosemary, coarsely ground black pepper, and fresh sea salt. A grill rack makes flipping the bass even easier.

INGREDIENTS

½ large orange, juiced

2 whole striped bass, about 2 pounds each, gutted, cleaned, fins removed

2 sprigs rosemary, leaves removed

Coarsely ground black pepper

Fresh sea salt

1 Grab the orange half and squeeze over the whole striped bass. Next, season with the rosemary leaves, coarsely ground black pepper, and fresh sea salt. Cover with aluminum foil and let rest at room temperature for about 1 hour.

2 Preheat your gas or charcoal grill to medium-high heat.

3 When the grill is ready, at about 450 to 500 degrees with the coals lightly covered with ash, place the whole striped bass on the grill for about 6 to 7 minutes, then flip. Finish cooking the fish for another 6 to 7 minutes, until the fish is juicy and opaque in the middle.

4 Remove the striped bass from the grill and transfer to a large cutting board. Cover and let rest for 5 to 10 minutes before serving.

Marinades

In general, you'll find that the central ingredient to a successful marinade is time. Most of the fundamental marinades that follow don't require too much prep time. Over the past several summers, I've spent many afternoons thinking of the next day's meal, thinking of which meat I'd be ordering, thinking of which marinade I'd be working with. If you work a 9-to-5 job like I do, you'll quickly realize that planning ahead is absolutely necessary when you work with marinades. Having your meat in the refrigerator marinating before you head off to the office is the best way to do it, though some meats you may want to marinate through the night!

There really is no such thing as marinating for too long. Take that with a grain of salt and don't start marinating for a week's length of time, as your meat will definitely go bad. However, when you see the marinating times for each recipe, understand that this is at the low end of the time spectrum. In general, if you have the time, marinate longer. The longer you marinate, the more your meat will gradually take on your desired flavors.

Unlike rubs and sauces, marinades can be a much gentler and a more delicate flavor-booster. Since most meats (not so much with seafood) often don't take on too much of the marinade's flavor (unless you're working with an Asian marinade such as teriyaki), you have much more room to experiment. Your meat is flexible and forgiving when it comes to marinades, and you'll also find that the simple combinations—such as a red wine and rosemary marinade for red meat, or a white wine, thyme, and lemon juice marinade for poultry and seafood—are real crowd-pleasers.

Teriyaki Marinade

1 In a bowl, combine all of the ingredients until the sugar has dissolved completely.

2 Apply marinade to meat immediately, and marinate for at least 4 hours.

INGREDIENTS

½ cup soy sauce

¼ cup brown sugar

2 tablespoons rice vinegar

2 garlic cloves, minced

2 teaspoons ginger, minced

1 teaspoon ground black pepper

Olive Oil and Garlic Marinade

INGREDIENTS

12 garlic cloves, crushed

6 sprigs rosemary, leaves removed

4 sprigs thyme, leaves removed

2½ cups extra-virgin olive oil

1 tablespoon coarsely ground black pepper

1 tablespoon fresh sea salt

1 Add all the ingredients of the marinade into a large bowl, large enough to hold the meat comfortably. Transfer the marinade into the refrigerator and let stand for about 45 minutes.

2 Add the meat into the marinade and let marinate for 2 hours in the refrigerator. If the meat isn't fully submerged in the marinade, rotate it a couple of times.

3 A half hour before roasting, remove the meat from the marinade and place on the roasting rack so that the marinade seeps from the meat.

Red Wine and Dijon Marinade

1 Add all of the ingredients to a large bowl that will be able to hold the meat. Transfer the marinade into the refrigerator and let stand for about 45 minutes.

2 Add the meat into the marinade and let marinate for 2 hours in the refrigerator. If the meat isn't fully submerged in the marinade, rotate it a couple of times.

3 A half hour before roasting, remove the meat from the marinade and place on the roasting rack so that the marinade seeps from the meat.

4 While cooking, baste the rib roast with the remaining marinade about every half hour.

INGREDIENTS

¾ cup dry red wine

¼ cup extra-virgin olive oil

2 garlic cloves, minced

1 tablespoon Dijon mustard

1 tablespoon coarsely ground black pepper

1 tablespoon fresh sea salt

1 teaspoon rosemary, finely chopped

Apple Cider Marinade

WORKS BEST WITH: ☐ RED MEAT ☑ PORK ☑ POULTRY ☐ SEAFOOD

FLAVOR: ☐ SPICY ☑ SWEET ☐ TANGY ☑ SAVORY ☐ SALTY

INGREDIENTS

2 cups fresh apple cider

¼ cup olive oil

½ lemon, juiced

2 sprigs thyme, leaves removed and finely chopped

2 sprigs rosemary, leaves removed and finely chopped

2 garlic cloves, minced

1 tablespoon coarsely ground black pepper

2 teaspoons fresh sea salt

1 In a medium bowl or roasting pan, combine all the ingredients to the marinade and let rest for 15 minutes for the flavors to spread throughout the marinade.

2 Add your desired meat into the marinade. Transfer to the refrigerator and let marinate from 4 hours to overnight. If the marinade does not fully cover the meat, turn the meat halfway through the marinating process so that all areas of the meat receive equal amounts of the marinade.

Lemon-Rosemary Marinade

WORKS BEST WITH: ☐ RED MEAT ☑ PORK ☑ POULTRY ☑ SEAFOOD

FLAVOR: ☐ SPICY ☐ SWEET ☑ TANGY ☑ SAVORY ☐ SALTY

1 In a medium bowl, combine all the ingredients and let rest for 15 minutes for the flavors to spread throughout the marinade.

2 Add the meat into the marinade. Transfer to the refrigerator and let marinate for about 4 hours. If the marinade does not fully cover the meat, turn the meat halfway through the marinating process so that all areas of the meat receive equal amounts of the marinade.

INGREDIENTS

4 lemons, halved and juiced

6 garlic cloves

3 sprigs fresh thyme, leaves removed

3 sprigs fresh rosemary, leaves removed

2 teaspoons ground fennel

1 tablespoon coarsely ground black pepper

1 tablespoon fresh sea salt

Pineapple Marinade

INGREDIENTS

1½ cups pineapple juice

¼ cup brown sugar

¼ cup soy sauce

2 garlic cloves, minced

1 teaspoon sea salt

1 In a bowl, combine all of the ingredients until the sugar has dissolved completely.

2 Place meat in marinade and marinate for at least 30 minutes.

Balsamic Marinade

WORKS BEST WITH: ☑ RED MEAT ☑ PORK ☐ POULTRY ☐ SEAFOOD

FLAVOR: ☐ SPICY ☑ SWEET ☑ TANGY ☐ SAVORY ☐ SALTY

1 In a medium bowl or roasting pan, combine all the marinade ingredients and let rest for 15 minutes in order for the flavors to spread throughout the marinade.

2 Add your desired meat into the marinade. Transfer to the refrigerator and let marinate from 4 hours to overnight. The marinade may not fully cover the meat. In that case, turn the meat halfway through the marinating process so that all areas of the meat receive equal amounts of the marinade.

INGREDIENTS

4 sprigs fresh basil

2 sprigs fresh rosemary, leaves removed

2 garlic cloves, crushed

2 teaspoons Dijon mustard

1 teaspoon raw honey

1 cup olive oil

¼ cup balsamic vinegar

1 tablespoon coarsely ground black pepper

1 tablespoon fresh sea salt

Mint Marinade

INGREDIENTS

½ cup olive oil

½ cup fresh mint leaves, finely chopped

¼ cup dry red wine

4 garlic cloves, finely chopped

1 tablespoon fresh parsley, finely chopped

1 tablespoon coarsely ground black pepper

2 teaspoons fresh sea salt

1 In a medium bowl or roasting pan, combine all the marinade ingredients and let rest for 15 minutes in order for the flavors to spread throughout the marinade.

2 Add your desired meat into the marinade. Transfer to the refrigerator and let marinate from 4 hours to overnight. Note that the marinade may not fully cover the meat. In that case, turn the meat halfway through the marinating process so that all areas of the meat receive equal amounts of the marinade.

Cilantro-Lime Marinade

1 In a medium bowl or roasting pan, combine all the marinade ingredients and let rest for 15 minutes for the flavors to spread throughout the marinade.

2 Add your desired meat into the marinade. Transfer to the refrigerator and let marinate from 4 hours to overnight. If the marinade does not fully cover the meat, turn the meat halfway through the marinating process so that all areas of the meat receive equal amounts of the marinade.

INGREDIENTS

2 limes, juiced

¼ cup olive oil

¼ cup fresh cilantro, finely chopped

2 garlic cloves, finely chopped

2 teaspoons coarsely ground black pepper

2 teaspoons fresh sea salt

½ teaspoon organic honey

Citrus Marinade

INGREDIENTS

¾ cup orange juice

½ medium lime, juiced

½ medium lemon, juiced

¼ cup cilantro, finely chopped

¼ cup extra-virgin olive oil

2 tablespoons rosemary, finely chopped

4 garlic cloves, minced

1 tablespoon coarsely ground black pepper

1 tablespoon fresh sea salt

1 Put all the marinade ingredients in a bowl large enough to also accommodate the meat. If the meat isn't fully submerged in the marinade, rotate it a couple of times.

2 Add the meat into the marinade and let marinate for 2 hours in the refrigerator. The meat will not be fully submerged in the marinade, so be sure to rotate it throughout the marinating process in order for all sides of the roast to receive equal marinating time.

3 A half hour before roasting, remove the meat from the marinade and place on the roasting rack so that the marinade seeps from the meat. Discard the remaining marinade.

Five-Spice Marinade

1 In a bowl, combine all of the ingredients until they are well mixed.

2 Apply marinade to meat immediately, and marinate for at least 4 hours.

INGREDIENTS

¾ cup soy sauce

¼ cup vinegar

2 tablespoons fresh ginger, minced

2 teaspoons sesame oil

2 teaspoons five-spice powder

¼ cup olive oil

1 teaspoon ground black pepper

Ginger-Sesame Marinade

INGREDIENTS

½ cup soy sauce

1 tablespoon fresh ginger, grated

1 tablespoon sesame oil

2 teaspoons sesame seeds

4 scallions, chopped

1 teaspoon ground black pepper

Combine all of the ingredients into a bowl and serve immediately.

Tandoori Marinade

1 In a small skillet, heat the olive oil over medium heat. Add the spices (everything aside from the lime juice and yogurt) to the skillet and toast for 2 minutes. The spices, with the olive oil, should form a paste. If not, add more olive oil to the mixture.

2 Transfer the toasted spices to a bowl and stir in the lime juice and yogurt. Place your meat in the marinade for at least 3 hours before grilling.

INGREDIENTS

2 tablespoons olive oil

2 garlic cloves, minced

½ teaspoon ground turmeric

2 tablespoons cumin powder

1 tablespoon fresh ginger, minced

1 teaspoon paprika

1 teaspoon coriander seeds

3 tablespoons cilantro, minced

½ small lime, juiced

1½ cups plain yogurt

Adobo Marinade

INGREDIENTS

1 can chipotle in adobo
(7 ounces)

2 garlic cloves, minced

½ small lime, juiced

1 teaspoon ground
black pepper

1 teaspoon sea salt

Add all of the ingredients to a blender, and then pulse to the desired consistency. Remove and marinate meat immediately.

Jamaican Jerk Marinade

Place all of the ingredients into a blender, and then pulse to the desired consistency. Remove and marinate meat immediately.

VARIATION: For a smokier flavor, consider adding 1 or 2 teaspoons of liquid smoke to the ingredients. I recommend Colgin's.

INGREDIENTS

1 medium onion, finely chopped

¼ cup scallions, finely chopped

1 scotch bonnet pepper, chopped

3 tablespoons soy sauce

1 tablespoon white vinegar

3 tablespoons olive oil

2 teaspoons thyme leaves, chopped

2 teaspoons sugar

1 teaspoon sea salt

1 teaspoon ground black pepper

1 teaspoon allspice

½ teaspoon nutmeg

½ teaspoon cinnamon

Steak Marinade

INGREDIENTS

4 garlic cloves, finely chopped

1 tablespoon Dijon mustard

1 tablespoon soy sauce

1 tablespoon olive oil

1 tablespoon Worcestershire sauce

2 teaspoons ground black pepper

1 teaspoon sea salt

1 In a bowl, combine all of the ingredients and stir until the desired consistency has been reached.

2 Marinate meat for at least 1 hour.

VARIATION: For a smokier flavor, consider adding 1 or 2 teaspoons of liquid smoke to the ingredients. I recommend Colgin's.

Carne Asada Marinade

1 In a bowl, combine all of the ingredients and stir until the desired consistency has been reached.

2 Marinate meat for at least 1 hour.

INGREDIENTS

2 limes, juiced

4 garlic cloves, minced

¾ cup orange juice

1 cup cilantro, chopped

1 tablespoon soy sauce

1 teaspoon ground coriander

1 tablespoon sea salt

1 tablespoon ground black pepper

¼ cup olive oil

10-Minute All-Purpose Marinade

WORKS BEST WITH: ☑ RED MEAT ☑ PORK ☑ POULTRY ☑ SEAFOOD

FLAVOR: ☐ SPICY ☐ SWEET ☐ TANGY ☑ SAVORY ☐ SALTY

INGREDIENTS

½ cup soy sauce

2 tablespoons Worcestershire sauce

2 garlic cloves, finely chopped

¼ medium onion, finely chopped

¼ cup olive oil

½ lime, juiced

1 In a bowl, combine all of the ingredients and stir until the desired consistency has been reached.

2 Marinate meat for at least 1 hour.

Simple Poultry Brine

WORKS BEST WITH: ☐ RED MEAT ☐ PORK ☑ POULTRY ☐ SEAFOOD

FLAVOR: ☐ SPICY ☐ SWEET ☐ TANGY ☐ SAVORY ☐ SALTY

1 In a deep pot, combine all of the ingredients and stir until the desired consistency has been reached.

2 Add your poultry to the pot, and let marinate at room temperature for 2 to 3 hours.

INGREDIENTS

1 gallon warm water

1 cup sea salt

1 cup light brown sugar

¼ cup olive oil

½ small lemon, juiced

4 garlic cloves, crushed

1 tablespoon ground black pepper

Basic Pork Brine

WORKS BEST WITH: ☐ RED MEAT ☑ PORK ☐ POULTRY ☐ SEAFOOD

FLAVOR: ☐ SPICY ☐ SWEET ☐ TANGY ☐ SAVORY ☑ SALTY

INGREDIENTS

1 gallon warm water

¼ cup apple cider vinegar

¼ cup light brown sugar

1 teaspoon thyme, minced

5 garlic cloves, minced

½ small lemon, juiced

1 tablespoon ground black pepper

2 tablespoons sea salt

1 In a deep pot, combine all of the ingredients and stir until the desired consistency has been reached.

2 Add your pork to the pot, and let marinate at room temperature for 2 to 3 hours.

Cooking with Marinades

Grilled Calamari

MAKES 6 SERVINGS • **ACTIVE TIME: 15 MINUTES** • **TOTAL TIME: 2 HOURS**

This classy appetizer is best served family style.

TOOLS

Cast-iron skillet

INGREDIENTS

1 lemon, juiced

¼ cup olive oil

2 garlic cloves, finely chopped

2 sprigs fresh oregano, leaves removed

Coarsely ground black pepper

Fresh sea salt

2 pounds fresh squid, tentacles separated from bodies

Marinara sauce for dipping, warmed

1 Combine the lemon juice, olive oil, garlic, and oregano in a large bowl. Season with coarsely ground black pepper and fresh sea salt. Add the squid to the bowl and let marinate for 1 to 2 hours.

2 Prepare your gas or charcoal grill to medium-high heat. Leave a cast-iron skillet on the grill while heating so that it develops a faint, smoky flavor.

3 When the grill is ready, at about 400 degrees with the coals lightly covered with ash, place the squid tentacles and rings on the grill and cook until opaque, about 2 to 3 minutes. When finished, transfer the squid to a large carving board and let stand at room temperature for 5 minutes before serving with warm marinara sauce on the side.

Tri-Tip Steak Marinated

MAKES 3 SERVINGS • ACTIVE TIME: 45 MINUTES • TOTAL TIME: 14 HOURS

The tri-tip is great for large gatherings in the summer since everyone can pick and choose as much meat as they want!

with Red Wine and Herbs

1 The day before grilling, combine the marinade ingredients in a large sealable plastic bag. Let rest at room temperature for 20 minutes, then add the tri-tip roast to the bag so that it is completely submerged; more wine may be necessary. Seal and place in the refrigerator and let marinate overnight.

2 One hour before grilling, remove the tri-tip bag from the refrigerator and let stand at room temperature.

3 Prepare your gas or charcoal grill, designating two sections: one for direct medium-high heat and the other for indirect heat. To do this, simply arrange the coals toward one side of the grill.

4 When the grill is ready, at about 400 to 450 degrees with the coals lightly covered with ash, remove the steaks from the marinade and grill over direct heat for about 5 minutes per side. Next, move the steaks to the indirect heat and cover the grill. Cook for another 20 to 30 minutes, flipping every 5 minutes.

5 Remove the steaks from the grill and transfer to a large cutting board. Let stand for 10 minutes, allowing the steaks to properly store their juices and flavor, and then slice across the grain into thin slices. Serve warm.

MARINADE INGREDIENTS

2 cups red wine

2 tablespoons red wine vinegar

2 garlic cloves, crushed

2 sprigs rosemary, leaves removed and minced

2 sprigs thyme, leaves removed and minced

½ small white onion, finely chopped

1 teaspoon fresh lemon juice

½ teaspoon dried oregano

Coarsely ground black pepper

Fresh sea salt

STEAK INGREDIENTS

1 tri-tip roast, about 1½ inches thick and 2 to 2½ pounds

TIP: IT IS IMPORTANT TO NOTE THAT THIS DISH REQUIRES MARINATING OVERNIGHT SO THAT IT SOFTENS AND BECOMES MORE TENDER ON THE GRILL.

Butcher's Steak

MAKES 2 SERVINGS • **ACTIVE TIME: 15 MINUTES**
TOTAL TIME: 1 HOUR AND 30 MINUTES

I first heard of this steak in a review of the restaurant St. Anselm in Brooklyn, New York. Aside from the tremendous reviews, I went to this restaurant because my father and brother both attended St. Anselm College in Manchester, New Hampshire. The butcher's steak, or the hanger steak, is such a phenomenal piece of meat when cooked properly. Be sure to marinate this dish in oil beforehand so that the steak is charred and gristly after grilling.

MARINADE INGREDIENTS

3 cups olive oil

6 cloves garlic, crushed

3 sprigs rosemary

3 sprigs thyme

¼ lemon, juiced

STEAK INGREDIENTS

2 hanger steaks, about 1 to ½ pounds each

Coarsely ground black pepper

Fresh sea salt

1 Mix the marinade ingredients in a small, rectangular dish. Lay the steaks into the dish so that the marinade completely covers the steaks. If not, add more olive oil until it does. Cover with aluminum foil and place in the refrigerator and let rest for at least 4 hours.

2 Remove the steaks from the refrigerator and let stand at room temperature for about 1 hour.

3 A half hour before cooking, prepare your gas or charcoal grill to medium-high heat.

4 When the grill is ready, at about 400 to 450 degrees with the coals lightly covered with ash, remove the steaks from the marinade and season with the coarsely ground pepper and sea salt. Set the marinade aside.

5 Place the seasoned side of the steak on the grill. Cook for about 4 to 5 minutes, basting the steaks with the remaining marinade every 30 seconds. When the steak is charred, gently flip and cook for 3 to 4 more minutes for medium-rare or 5 more minutes for medium. The steaks should feel slightly firm if poked in the center.

6 Remove the steaks from the grill and transfer to a large cutting board. Let stand for 5 to 10 minutes, allowing the steaks to properly store their juices and flavor. Serve warm.

Marinated Steak Kebabs with Salsa Verde and Grilled Cherry Tomatoes

MAKES 3 TO 4 SERVINGS • ACTIVE TIME: 45 MINUTES • TOTAL TIME: 4 HOURS

Even kids love meat on a stick. But the salsa verde will please the adults in the crowd.

TOOLS

Skewers

SALSA VERDE INGREDIENTS

1 cup fresh Italian parsley leaves

½ cup fresh cilantro

¼ very small shallot

1 anchovy fillet

1 tablespoon capers

2 garlic cloves

1 teaspoon red wine vinegar

½ cup olive oil

KEBAB INGREDIENTS

2 to 3 pounds top sirloin

1 cup olive oil

¼ cup fresh basil leaves

1 sprig rosemary, leaves removed

1 garlic clove, minced

1 bag skewers

TOMATO INGREDIENTS

3 tablespoons olive oil

8 to 12 cherry tomatoes, still on vine

1 sprig thyme, leaves removed

Coarsely ground black pepper

Continued on next page >

< Continued from previous page

1 Cut the top sirloin into 1½- to 2-inch cubes. Combine the olive oil, basil leaves, rosemary, and garlic in a large sealable bag, then add the cuts of meat. Seal tight and let rest at room temperature for 2 to 3 hours.

2 A half hour before cooking, prepare your gas or charcoal grill to medium-high heat.

3 When the sirloin cuts have finished marinating, remove from bag and take 3 to 4 pieces of meat and pierce with the skewers.

4 Drizzle the olive oil over the tomatoes in a bowl and sprinkle with thyme. Season with black pepper. Set aside.

5 In a small food processor, add the parsley, cilantro, shallot, anchovy, capers, garlic cloves, and red wine vinegar. Pulse into a thick paste. Remove from processor and place into a small bowl. Whisk in the olive oil and set aside.

6 When the grill is ready, at about 400 degrees with the coals lightly covered with ash, place the kebabs on the grill. Grill the kebabs for about 8 to 9 minutes for medium-rare, 10 minutes for medium. Rotate the kebabs about every 2 minutes so each side is cooked evenly. After 4 minutes, add the oiled tomatoes and cook until the skin is a little crispy and blistered.

7 Remove kebabs and tomatoes from grill and transfer to a large cutting board. Let rest for 5 minutes and serve warm with salsa verde.

> **TIP:** SALSA VERDE CAN BE REFRIGERATED OVERNIGHT AND SERVED ALONGSIDE A DIFFERENT CUT OF STEAK, CHICKEN, OR PORK!

Beer-Marinated Prime Rib

Beer is the perfect marinade for any cut of red meat. Since the rib roast has a dense core, the marinade will mostly penetrate the roast's cap, with a little flavor making its way to the core. Serve this with a porter or stout.

1 Place the rib roast meat side down in a large bowl or baking pan—something large enough to hold the rib roast. Generously season the meat with the coarsely ground black pepper and fresh sea salt, massaging it in with your hands and making sure that the seasoning thoroughly sticks to the roast.

2 Mix the minced garlic and 2 teaspoons of extra-virgin olive oil in a small cup, and then brush onto the rib roast over the pepper and salt.

3 Add the remaining ingredients into the baking pan and mix thoroughly. Note that the entire rib roast will not be submerged in the marinade—part of the reason why we want to keep the rib roast meat side down in the baking pan—so be sure to spoon the marinade onto the rib side of the roast throughout the marinating process.

Continued on next page >

INGREDIENTS

A 6-rib rib roast

3 tablespoons coarsely ground black pepper

2 tablespoons fresh sea salt

4 garlic cloves, minced

¼ cup, plus 2 teaspoons extra-virgin olive oil

4 sprigs fresh rosemary

4 sprigs fresh thyme

2 tablespoons soy sauce

1 teaspoon Worcestershire sauce

2 cups dark beer (e.g., brown ale, dark stout)

1 large white onion, diced

< Continued from previous page

4 Transfer the baking dish into the refrigerator and let marinate for about 4 hours. Remove roast from the marinade and transfer to a large carving board 1 hour before roasting. Set the marinade aside; it will be used for basting during the roasting process.

5 Preheat the oven to 425 degrees.

6 Place the rib roast meat side up on a rack in the roasting pan. Lightly season again with the coarsely ground black pepper and fresh sea salt. When the oven is ready, transfer the rib roast to the oven and cook for 15 minutes at 450 degrees so that it gets a strong initial searing.

7 Reduce the heat to 325 degrees and continue to roast for about 3 to 4 more hours. Baste with the marinade every 30 minutes or so during the roasting process. Use the juices and marinade that accumulate at the bottom of the roasting pan as a strong base for an au jus (page 226 to 229).

8 Remove the rib roast from the oven and let stand for 15 minutes before carving, allowing it to properly store its juices and flavor.

Leg of Lamb with Rosemary-Mustard Marinade

MAKES 4 SERVINGS • **ACTIVE TIME: 30 MINUTES** • **TOTAL TIME: 1 HOUR**

The flavors of the rosemary and mustard work well when paired with a leg of lamb. In addition, note that the variation here encourages you to smoke the lamb, allowing for the rich flavor of the mustard to be more pronounced and soulful.

INGREDIENTS

3 tablespoons olive oil

¼ cup rosemary leaves, finely chopped

¼ cup Dijon mustard

4 garlic cloves, finely chopped

1 large shallot, finely chopped

¼ small lemon, juiced

1 tablespoon flat-leaf parsley, finely chopped

Coarsely ground black pepper

Fresh sea salt

A 6-pound boneless leg of lamb, butterflied

Continued on next page >

< Continued from previous page

1 In a small bowl, whisk together the olive oil, rosemary, mustard, garlic, shallot, parsley, pepper, and salt.

2 Place the leg of lamb on a roasting rack. Setting a little aside, rub the marinade on the lamb, massaging it thoroughly into crevices of the meat. Cover the lamb with a sheet of aluminum foil and let stand at room temperature for about 2 hours.

3 A half hour before grilling, prepare your gas or charcoal grill to medium-high heat.

4 When the coals are ready, at about 400 degrees with the coals lightly covered with ash, place the marinated leg of lamb on the grill and cook for about 16 minutes per side for medium-rare, 17 minutes for medium. While grilling, brush the remaining marinade on top of the lamb. When finished, transfer the lamb to a large carving board and let rest for 15 minutes, allowing for the meat to properly store its juices.

5 Before serving, slice the lamb into ½-inch-thick diagonal strips. Serve warm. Consider garnishing with wedges of lemon and parsley leaves.

VARIATION: An hour before grilling, take 2 to 3 cups of hickory or oak woodchips and soak them in water. Just before you place the lamb on the grill, scatter the woodchips over the coals. Cover the grill so that the smoke pillows around the meat, and then cook for about 15 minutes for medium-rare.

Marinated Lamb Kebabs with Mint Chimichurri

**MAKES 8 TO 10 SERVINGS • ACTIVE TIME: 30 MINUTES
TOTAL TIME: 5 TO 13 HOURS**

Lamb kebabs are perfect for a large gathering, which is why this recipe is for 8 to 10 servings. You have to try the mint chimichurri with lamb!

TOOLS

Food processor

24 bamboo skewers

MINT CHIMICHURRI INGREDIENTS

2 garlic cloves

2 cups fresh flat-leaf parsley

2 cups fresh mint leaves

1 small shallot

¼ small lime, juiced

4 tablespoons red wine vinegar

½ cup olive oil

Coarsely ground black pepper

Fresh sea salt

KEBAB INGREDIENTS

2 pounds lamb, cut into 1½-inch cubes

Coarsely ground black pepper

Fresh sea salt

3 tablespoons olive oil

1½ cups red wine

4 garlic cloves, crushed

1 shallot, finely chopped

2 teaspoons rosemary, finely chopped

1 teaspoon ground cumin

2 red onions, cut into square pieces

2 red peppers, cut into square pieces

Continued on next page >

< Continued from previous page

1 The night before you plan to grill, season the lamb cubes with coarsely ground black pepper and fresh sea salt. Set aside.

2 In a large sealable plastic bag (if you need two, divide the recipe between both bags), combine the remaining lamb ingredients except for the onion and pepper. Add the lamb cubes to the bag and then transfer to the refrigerator, letting the meat marinate from 4 hours to overnight, the longer the better.

3 An hour and a half before grilling, remove the lamb from the refrigerator and let rest, uncovered and outside of the red wine marinade, at room temperature.

4 In a small food processor, purée the garlic, parsley, mint, shallot, lime juice, and red wine vinegar. Slowly beat in the olive oil and then remove from the processor. Season with coarsely ground black pepper and fresh sea salt, cover and then set aside.

5 A half hour before grilling, prepare your gas or charcoal grill to medium-high heat.

6 Pierce about four lamb cubes with each bamboo skewer, making sure to align the pieces of onion and pepper in between each cube.

7 When the grill is ready, at about 400 degrees with the coals lightly covered with ash, place the skewers on the grill and cook for about 15 to 20 minutes. Transfer the kebabs to a large carving board and let them rest for 5 minutes before serving with the mint chimichurri sauce.

Grilled Beef Short Ribs with

Beef short ribs are extremely soft and delicate after marinating. You can eat these with your hands, but set the table with forks and knives for the bits that fall off the bone.

Red Wine and Basil Marinade

1 The night before you plan on grilling, combine all the marinade ingredients except the wine in a large bowl or roasting pan. Add the short ribs and pour in the wine. Move the bowl to the refrigerator and let rest for 4 to 6 hours.

2 Transfer the ribs from the marinade to a large cutting board or plate and let stand at room temperature for 1 hour. Season one side of the ribs with pepper and salt.

3 A half hour before cooking, prepare your gas or charcoal grill to medium-high heat.

4 When the grill is ready, at about 400 to 450 degrees with the coals lightly covered with ash, place the seasoned sides of the ribs on the grill and cook for about 4 minutes. Season the tops of the ribs while waiting. When the steaks are charred, flip and cook for 4 more minutes.

5 Transfer the ribs to a cutting board and let rest for 5 to 10 minutes. Serve warm.

MARINADE INGREDIENTS

2 cups fresh basil leaves, finely chopped

2 large carrots, finely chopped

2 large onions, finely chopped

2 garlic cloves, finely chopped

1 scallion, finely chopped

2 sprigs thyme, leaves removed

2 sprigs rosemary, leaves removed

2 sprigs oregano, leaves removed

3 tablespoons olive oil

1 bottle dry red wine

SHORT RIB INGREDIENTS

3 to 4 pounds beef short ribs, meaty and cut into 3 to 5 inches

Coarsely ground black pepper

Fresh sea salt

Grilled Roast Pineapple Pork Loin

The exotic flavors of pineapple and ginger make for a guest-worthy variation on grilled pork loin.

INGREDIENTS

5 tablespoons olive oil

1 or 2 sprigs fresh rosemary

1 cup crushed pineapple

¼ cup honey

¼ cup water

1 teaspoon fresh ground
or grated ginger

2¼ pounds pork loin

Fresh sea salt

Freshly ground cracked pepper

Continued on next page >

< Continued from previous page

1 Fire up your grill and allow the coals to settle into a temperature of about 350 degrees.

2 While the grill is heating, slowly sauté the olive oil and rosemary in a cast-iron or All Clad–style high heat–friendly pan. Be sure the pan is oven friendly, as you will be placing this pan directly onto your grill.

3 After the oil and rosemary have been thoroughly heated and the flavors of the sprigs are infused throughout the oil, add in a $\frac{1}{2}$ cup crushed pineapple, honey, water, and ginger. Stir thoroughly, and bring the mixture to a soft boil.

4 Rub the pork loin with salt and pepper to your desired seasoning, and place the pork loin into the pan, turning it so the entire loin is covered with the basting sauce for 5 to 10 minutes at a medium heat until the loin begins to brown. Once your grill has reached the desired temperature, move the entire pan to your grill grate.

5 Cover your grill and allow the pork to cook for 45 minutes, turning and basting the pork occasionally so all sides are browned from the heat of the hot pan.

6 After about 45 minutes, remove the pork loin from the pan and place directly on the grate. Use the remaining $\frac{1}{2}$ cup of crushed pineapple to baste the loin thoroughly, creating a golden brown glaze as you turn the loin for another 15 minutes.

7 Remove from fire and let the loin rest for 10 to 12 minutes. Carve and serve!

Italian Pork

MAKES 4 TO 6 SERVINGS • ACTIVE TIME: 1 HOUR AND 30 MINUTES
TOTAL TIME: BE PREPARED TO MARINATE OVERNIGHT

We first experienced Italian pork porchetta sandwiches in a small market outside the center of Siena, Italy. The flavors were outstanding. I had two, the second with a slice of aged hard Parmesan cheese that I cut from a wedge that we purchased to enjoy later that afternoon. It was mind-blowing. We decided to recreate this amazing dish on our own, grilling the pork over apple wood to add that wonderful smoked flavor to an already extraordinarily tasty recipe.

1 Allow the pork to achieve room temperature. Season the pork shoulder with salt and pepper to taste.

2 In a large sauce pan, heat the olive oil and the oil from the anchovies together over high heat. Toss in the garlic and onions and cook until they are near brown. Stir in the rosemary, crushed red pepper, fennel seeds, the zest of 1 orange and 1 lemon, and 3 or 4 fillets of anchovies. Use a wood spatula and break down the anchovy fillets as you stir and mix the ingredients, creating your marinade. About a minute before you remove the sauce pan from the grill or stovetop, pour in the freshly squeezed orange juice and stir so the sweet citric flavor merges throughout. Remove the pan and allow this mixture to cool to room temperature.

3 Season the bottom of a glass casserole dish with the marinade and rest the pork shoulder into this dish. Use the remaining marinade to completely cover the pork shoulder, spreading and massaging the marinade into the various nooks and crannies of the meat. Cover the dish and refrigerate overnight.

Porchetta

4 Remove the pork from the refrigerator several hours before you plan to cook. Allow the marinated pork to achieve room temperature once more. Meanwhile, fire up your grill to about 300 to 400 degrees.

5 Place the pork shoulder directly on the preheated grill, pouring the excess marinade over it so the full flavors of the marinade can be cooked into the pork. (For health reasons, do NOT use this marinade later in the cooking process for basting; the marinade has had raw meat soaking in it, and it needs to cook just as the meat does.)

6 Cook the shoulder for about 6 to 8 minutes on either side, closing the grill so the smoke and heat will work together in an oven-like manner.

7 Once the pork has reached your desired temperature level (about 145 degrees for medium), remove it and allow it to cool for 10 to 15 minutes before slicing it thinly.

> **TIP:** WHILE THE PORK IS MARINATING, TURN IT OVER AT LEAST ONCE, EQUALLY DISTRIBUTING THE MARINADE.

INGREDIENTS

2½- to 3-pound boneless pork shoulder, butterflied

½ cup sea salt

½ cup freshly ground black pepper

2 or 3 tablespoons olive oil

Small tin olive oil–packed anchovies (use the oil)

4 cloves garlic, sliced paper thin

1 medium-size onion, chopped

Needles from 1 or 2 sprigs rosemary

2½ tablespoons crushed red pepper

1½ tablespoons fennel seeds

2 oranges (zest one completely; save the other to grill)

1 lemon (zest the entire rind)

Whole Marinated Chicken with Chipotle Cauliflower

For the marinade, be sure to let the bird soak for up to 6 hours, the longer the better. As for the chipotle cauliflower, if you would like to add a smoky flavor, throw some soaked woodchips over the coals and grill with the lid covered.

CHICKEN INGREDIENTS

½ cup olive oil for marinade plus 1 tablespoon for grilling

½ small white onion, finely chopped

¼ cup fresh flat-leaf parsley, finely chopped

2 sprigs rosemary, leaves removed and minced

2 garlic cloves, crushed

2 tablespoons red wine vinegar

A 4- to 5-pound whole chicken

Coarsely ground black pepper

Fresh sea salt

CAULIFLOWER INGREDIENTS

2 large heads cauliflower, cut into florets

¼ cup olive oil

½ lime, juiced

2 garlic cloves, diced

1 tablespoon chipotle powder

2 teaspoons paprika

2 tablespoons fresh basil leaves, sliced

Coarsely ground black pepper

Fresh sea salt

Continued on next page >

< Continued from previous page

1 In a large bowl, combine the olive oil, onion, parsley, rosemary, garlic, and vinegar and mix thoroughly. Add the chicken skin-side down to the marinade; keep in mind that the chicken will not be fully submerged. Let soak for 4 to 6 hours, turning the chicken with 1 hour remaining.

2 Remove the chicken from the marinade and season with pepper and salt. Let the chicken stand at room temperature for 30 minutes to 1 hour. A half hour before grilling, prepare your gas or charcoal grill to medium heat.

3 While waiting, mix the cauliflower florets, olive oil, and lime juice in a medium bowl. Stir in the remaining ingredients (garlic, chipotle powder, paprika, and basil) and season with ground pepper and salt. Transfer to a small frying pan. Set aside.

4 When the grill is ready, at about 400 degrees with the coals lightly covered with ash, place the chicken on the grill, skin-side up. Cover the grill and cook for about 40 minutes. Before flipping, brush the top of the chicken with 1 tablespoon of olive oil. Turn and cook for about 15 more minutes, until the skin is crisp and a meat thermometer, inserted into the thickest part of the thigh, reads 165 degrees.

5 Remove the chicken, transfer to a large cutting board, and let stand for 15 minutes.

6 Position the aluminum pan of cauliflower on the grill and cover with a lid. Cook for 8 to 9 minutes until the florets are crisp with the chipotle powder. Remove from grill and serve alongside the chicken.

Grilled Chicken with Arugula and Balsamic-Rosemary Vinaigrette

MAKES 4 SERVINGS • ACTIVE TIME: 25 MINUTES
TOTAL TIME: 2 HOURS AND 30 MINUTES

While grilling, baste the chicken thighs with the remaining marinade and keep the grill covered, allowing the skin to cook to a crisp.

INGREDIENTS

8 bone-in, skin-on chicken thighs

1 lemon, ½ juiced and ½ sliced into wedges

2 tablespoons Dijon mustard

3 sprigs rosemary, leaves removed from 2

1 garlic clove, finely chopped

½ cup, plus 4 tablespoons olive oil

2 tablespoons balsamic vinegar

¼ teaspoon red pepper flakes

Coarsely ground pepper

Fresh sea salt

4 cups arugula, stemmed

Continued on next page >

< Continued from previous page

1 Combine the chicken thighs, lemon juice, Dijon mustard, leaves from 2 rosemary sprigs, garlic, and 4 tablespoons of olive oil in a large sealable plastic bag. Seal and firmly mix with your hands. Let rest at room temperature for 2 hours.

2 A half hour before grilling, prepare your gas or charcoal grill to medium-high heat.

3 Add the remaining sprig of rosemary and $1/2$ cup of the olive oil to a small saucepan and set over medium-high heat. Bring to a simmer and then remove from heat. Discard the sprig of rosemary and pour the oil into a small bowl. Set aside.

4 When the coals are ready, at about 400 degrees with the coals lightly covered with ash, remove the chicken from the marinade and season with coarsely ground pepper and sea salt. Then, place the chicken thighs skin-side down on the grill, and let cook for about 9 minutes. Flip and cook for 4 to 5 more minutes. When finished, they should feel springy if poked with a finger.

5 Remove the chicken thighs from the grill and place on a large cutting board. Let rest for 5 to 10 minutes.

6 While waiting, mix the balsamic vinegar and red pepper flakes into the rosemary oil. Season with pepper and salt. Drizzle over arugula and plate evenly. Position chicken thighs on top of arugula salad and garnish with lemon wedges.

Jamaican Jerk Chicken with Smoked Pineapple

MAKES 4 SERVINGS • ACTIVE TIME: 45 MINUTES • TOTAL TIME: 26 HOURS

This is one of my favorite meals. The jerk spice on the chicken is intense and fiery and is not for the timid. And, bonus, Jamaican jerk chicken is just as good when served chilled the next day.

TOOLS

Food processor

2 to 3 cups hickory or oak woodchips

PINEAPPLE INGREDIENTS

1 pineapple, peeled, cored and cut into 1-inch thick rings

1 teaspoon dried thyme

Coarsely ground black pepper

Fresh sea salt

JERK CHICKEN INGREDIENTS

1 large yellow onion, halved

4 to 5 habanero chiles, stemmed and seeded

3 scallions

A 2-inch piece of ginger, peeled

8 garlic cloves

1 teaspoon ground cinnamon

1 teaspoon ground nutmeg

2 teaspoons allspice

1 teaspoon dried thyme

1 teaspoon cayenne

¼ teaspoon ground cloves

2 teaspoons coarsely ground black pepper

2 teaspoons fresh sea salt

½ small lime, juiced

½ cup olive oil

1½ cups warm water

4 bone-in, skin-on chicken thighs

4 skin-on chicken legs

Continued on next page >

< Continued from previous page

1 Combine all the chicken ingredients except the chicken itself in a food processor, and blend into a marinade. Remove the marinade and place into a large sealable plastic bag. Add the chicken thighs and legs, making sure they are fully submerged in the marinade. Refrigerate for a day—or two days, if you have the time.

2 Remove the bag from the refrigerator 1 hour before grilling. Transfer the chicken thighs and legs from the marinade onto a plate and let rest, uncovered, at room temperature for about 1 hour.

3 Soak the woodchips in water for 1 to 2 hours.

4 A half hour before grilling, prepare your gas or charcoal grill to medium heat. Designate two separate heat sections on the grill, one for direct-heat and the other for indirect-heat. To do this, simply arrange the coals toward one side of the grill.

5 While waiting, season the pineapple rings lightly with dried thyme, coarsely ground black pepper, and fresh sea salt, then transfer to beside the grill.

6 When the grill is ready, at about 350 to 400 degrees with the coals lightly covered with ash, remove the woodchips from the water and scatter over the coals. Place the pineapple rings over the cool side of the grill and cook for about 3 to 4 minutes on each side. When golden, remove from grill.

7 Place the chicken thighs and legs skin-side down on the grill over direct heat. Cover with the lid and grill for 6 to 7 minutes. Flip and move the thighs to the cool side of the grill. Cover again and grill for 4 to 5 more minutes. When finished, the chicken should feel springy if poked with a finger.

8 Remove the chicken from the grill and transfer to a large cutting board. Let rest for about 5 minutes, and then serve with the cooled pineapple.

Ginger-Sesame Chicken

MAKES 4 SERVINGS • ACTIVE TIME: 40 MINUTES
TOTAL TIME: 1 HOUR AND 30 MINUTES

Serving fresh-grilled Asian food on your porch or patio sure
beats takeout.

1 Heat 2 tablespoons of the olive oil in a small skillet over medium-high heat. When hot, add the ginger, onion, garlic, and lemon juice and sauté for about 2 to 3 minutes, or until the onions are translucent and the garlic is crisp but not browned. Remove from heat and transfer to a small bowl.

2 Rub the chicken breasts with pepper and salt and put them in a medium sealable plastic bag. Add the ginger-onion mixture and press around the chicken breasts. Seal and let rest at room temperature for 30 minutes.

3 Prepare your gas or charcoal grill to medium-high heat.

4 In a small dish, mix ½ teaspoon of the remaining olive oil with sesame seeds. Set aside.

5 When the grill is ready, about 400 to 450 degrees and the coals are lightly covered with ash, place the chicken on the grill and sprinkle the tops with half of the oiled sesame seeds. Grill the chicken breasts for about 7 minutes. Flip and season with the remaining sesame seeds, and then grill for 5 to 6 more minutes. When finished, they should feel springy if poked with a finger.

6 Remove and let rest for 5 minutes. Serve warm.

INGREDIENTS

2 tablespoons, plus ½ teaspoon olive oil

A 1- to 2-inch piece ginger, peeled and sliced

2 green onions, finely chopped

2 garlic cloves, minced

½ small lemon, juiced

4 boneless chicken breasts, about 1½ to 2 pounds

Coarsely ground black pepper

Fresh sea salt

3 tablespoons sesame seeds

Cilantro-Lime Chicken Tacos

MAKES 4 SERVINGS • ACTIVE TIME: 30 MINUTES
TOTAL TIME: 3 HOURS

Serve this dish—a personal favorite—on a warm summer night with a glass of sangria.

TACO INGREDIENTS

¾ cup fresh cilantro, finely chopped

2 limes, grated and juiced

½ cup olive oil

1 teaspoon red pepper flakes

2 teaspoons coarsely ground black pepper

1 teaspoon fresh sea salt

4 to 5 skinless, boneless chicken breasts

GUACAMOLE

2 large Mexican Hass avocados, halved and pitted

½ small lime, juiced

¼ small white onion, finely chopped

¼ to ½ cup fresh cilantro, chopped

1 jalapeño, stemmed, seeded, and finely chopped

Coarsely ground black pepper

Fresh sea salt

TOPPINGS

1 head iceberg or butter lettuce, leaves removed

2 to 3 cups cherry tomatoes, quartered

½ white onion, chopped

1 cup salsa verde (pages 165–166)

with Spicy Guacamole

1 Combine all the chicken ingredients in a sealable plastic bag and zip it closed. Rub the marinade around in the bag so that it is evenly distributed across the chicken breasts. Marinate in refrigerator for at least 2 hours, or overnight if you prefer.

2 Remove the chicken from the refrigerator and place, uncovered, on a large cutting board. Let rest for 30 minutes to 1 hour.

3 While waiting, prepare the toppings and place in small, individual bowls so that everyone will be able to pick and choose what they desire! Cover and place on table.

4 A half hour before grilling, prepare your gas or charcoal grill to medium heat.

5 When the grill is ready, about 400 to 450 degrees with the coals lightly covered with ash, place the chicken breasts on the grill and cook for about 7 minutes. When the bottom seems charred, flip the chicken and grill for another 5 to 6 minutes; they should feel springy if poked with a finger.

6 Transfer the chicken from the grill to a large cutting board and let rest for 10 to 15 minutes, allowing the meat to properly store its juices.

7 While the chicken rests, grab your guacamole ingredients and add to a large mortar (a medium bowl will do) and break apart with a pestle or fork. Combine the ingredients coarsely, making sure that there are still medium-sized pieces of avocado remaining.

8 Carve the chicken into small $1/4$-inch pieces and place into beds of iceberg or butter leaves. Serve with a scoop of guacamole to the side.

Smoked Ginger Chicken Satay with Almond Dipping Sauce

MAKES 5 SERVINGS • ACTIVE TIME: 30 MINUTES
TOTAL TIME: 2 HOURS AND 30 MINUTES

The smoked ginger chicken is perfect when served with almond dipping sauce, a strong substitute for classic peanut sauce.

CHICKEN SATAY INGREDIENTS

10 boneless, skinless chicken thighs, cut into small strips

A 1- to 2-inch piece of ginger, thinly sliced

2 tablespoons sesame seeds

1 large shallot, finely chopped

3 garlic cloves

1 teaspoon ground coriander

1 chile pepper of your choice, stemmed

2 teaspoons coarsely ground black pepper

1 teaspoon fresh sea salt

¼ cup olive oil

TOOLS

2 to 3 cups hickory or oak woodchips

1 bag bamboo skewers

ALMOND DIPPING SAUCE INGREDIENTS

½ cup almond butter

1½ cups coconut milk

1 wedge of lime, juiced

1 tablespoon fish sauce

½ teaspoon coarsely ground black pepper

½ teaspoon fresh sea salt

Continued on next page >

< Continued from previous page

1 Add all of the chicken satay ingredients into a sealable plastic bag and zip it closed, making sure that the marinade covers the chicken strips. Rub the marinade around the chicken in the bag and transfer to the refrigerator. Let marinate for 2 hours.

2 In a medium bowl, add the woodchips and submerge with water. Let soak for 1 hour.

3 Prepare your gas or charcoal grill to medium heat.

4 Remove the chicken strips from the marinade and pierce with the bamboo skewers. Reserve the marinade and place with the chicken strips alongside the grill.

5 Combine the ingredients for the almond dipping sauce in a small saucepan over medium-high heat and bring to a boil. Let cook for about 3 to 4 minutes until the sauce turns golden brown. Remove from heat and cover with aluminum foil.

6 When the grill is ready, about 400 degrees with the coals lightly covered with ash, scatter the woodchips over the coals. Wait a few minutes for the smoke to build, and then place the skewered chicken strips over the smoke. Cover the grill, aligning the vent away from the coals so that the smoke rolls over the chicken strips, and cook for about 4 minutes on each side.

7 Remove from heat and serve alongside the warm almond dipping sauce.

Brined and Grill-

**MAKES 8 TO 10 SERVINGS • ACTIVE TIME: 3 HOURS
TOTAL TIME: 9 TO 24 HOURS**

Brining and grilling poultry often go hand in hand, allowing for the meat to retain its juice and stay moist. To brine thoroughly, the bird must soak in a mixture of water and kosher salt for up to 12 hours, the longer the better. At the Whalen house for Thanksgiving, my father always does the traditional turkey in the oven and then this recipe with the rotisserie (optional) on the grill. Without a doubt, this is always the winning turkey. Serve with cranberry sauce (pages 102-103).

Roasted Turkey

1 In a large stockpot, add the turkey and submerge with about 8 cups of water and ½ cup of kosher salt; if you need more water, make sure to increase the amount of kosher salt. Let the turkey brine at room temperature for 6 to 12 hours.

2 Remove the turkey and pat dry. Grab the orange halves and squeeze over the turkey and inside its cavity. Next, rub the clarified butter on the turkey's skin and season with coarsely ground black pepper and rosemary.

3 Prepare your gas or charcoal grill to medium-low heat and designate two separate heat sections on the grill, one for direct heat and the other for indirect. To do this, simply arrange the coals toward one side of the grill.

4 When the grill is ready, at about 350 to 400 degrees with the coals lightly covered with ash, place the turkey over indirect heat and grill for about $2\,^3/_4$ hours. While grilling, you want to replenish the coals and flip the turkey every 45 minutes. Insert a meat thermometer into the thickest part of the thigh; when the turkey is finished, the thermometer should read 165 degrees.

5 Remove the turkey from the grill and cover with aluminum foil. Let rest for 45 minutes to 1 hour before carving.

INGREDIENTS

A 12- to 14-pound turkey

8 cups cold water

½ cup kosher salt

2 oranges, halved

2 tablespoons clarified butter

½ sprig rosemary, leaves removed

Coarsely ground black pepper

Grilled Lime Mahi-Mahi and Smoked Green Beans

Because the mahi-mahi has such delicate flavors, it works with nearly any side or marinade. But here we pair it with smoked green beans with prosciutto and pine nuts.

MAHI-MAHI INGREDIENTS

½ cup olive oil

½ small lime, juiced

1 garlic clove, minced

1 teaspoon red pepper flakes

½ teaspoon cayenne pepper

4 mahi-mahi fillets

Coarsely ground black pepper

Fresh sea salt

GREEN BEANS INGREDIENTS

2 tablespoons olive oil

3 ounces prosciutto, ⅛-inch thick, sliced into cubes

¼ cup pine nuts

2 garlic cloves, finely chopped

2 to 3 pounds green beans, ends trimmed

¼ small lemon, juiced

Coarsely ground black pepper

Fresh sea salt

Continued on next page >

< Continued from previous page

1 In a medium roasting pan, combine the olive oil, lime juice, garlic, red pepper flakes, and cayenne pepper and mix thoroughly. Place the mahi-mahi fillets into the marinade and let stand at room temperature for 1 to 2 hours, flipping once.

2 A half hour before cooking, place a cast-iron skillet on your gas or charcoal grill and prepare to medium heat. Leave the grill covered while heating, as it will add a faint smoky flavor to the skillet.

3 When the grill is ready, at about 400 degrees with the coals lightly covered with ash, add the olive oil into the skillet. Wait until very hot, and then add the prosciutto and sear until browned. Next, stir in the pine nuts, and toast about 3 minutes. Stir in the garlic and green beans, then top with lemon juice. Season generously with coarsely ground black pepper and sea salt, and cook until the green beans are charred and blistered, about 10 minutes.

4 While the green beans cook, remove the mahi-mahi fillets from the marinade and place directly over the heat source. Cover the grill and cook for about 4 to 5 minutes per side, until the fillets are flakey and moist when touched with a fork.

5 Remove the fillets and green beans from the grill and serve immediately.

Grilled Lemon and Basil Swordfish Steaks with Citrus Salsa

**MAKES 4 SERVINGS • ACTIVE TIME: 40 MINUTES
TOTAL TIME: 1 HOUR AND 45 MINUTES**

Swordfish is often considered a meat lover's fish, and it's very filling. These swordfish steaks are delicious served with this citrus salsa.

SWORDFISH INGREDIENTS

½ lemon, juiced

¼ cup fresh basil leaves

1 garlic clove, minced

½ cup olive oil, plus extra for the grill

4 swordfish steaks, 1¼ to 1¾ inches thick

Coarsely ground black pepper

Fresh sea salt

CITRUS SALSA INGREDIENTS

1 cup ripe pineapple, diced

¼ cup fresh cucumber, diced

¼ cup ripe mango, diced

1 small shallot, chopped

2 tablespoons bell pepper (red, yellow, or orange), diced

1 tablespoon fresh cilantro, finely chopped

¼ small lime, juiced

½ teaspoon Tabasco sauce

Coarsely ground black pepper

Fresh sea salt

Continued on next page >

< Continued from previous page

1 In a medium bowl, combine the lemon juice, fresh basil leaves, and garlic. Whisk in the olive oil and then let the marinade infuse for 1 hour. Next, rub the oil over the swordfish steaks and then season with coarsely ground black pepper and sea salt. Let stand at room temperature while you prepare the grill and the citrus salsa.

2 Prepare your gas or charcoal grill to high heat.

3 While the grill heats, combine the pineapple, cucumber, mango, shallot, bell pepper, and cilantro in a large bowl. Stir in the lime juice and Tabasco sauce and then season with coarsely ground black pepper and sea salt. Transfer the bowl to the refrigerator and let chill.

4 When the grill is ready, at about 450 to 500 degrees with the coals lightly covered with ash, brush the grate with a little olive oil. Place the swordfish steaks on the grill and then grill for about 3 to 4 minutes per side, until the fish is opaque.

5 Remove the steaks from the grill and place on a large carving board. Let stand for 5 to 10 minutes, and then serve with a side of citrus salsa.

TIP: YOU WON'T NEED A WHOLE BELL PEPPER FOR THE CITRUS SALSA. GRILL THE REST OF THE PEPPER WHILE YOU'RE GRILLING THE SWORDFISH.

Grilled Trout with

MAKES 4 SERVINGS • ACTIVE TIME: 35 MINUTES
TOTAL TIME: 1 HOUR AND 10 MINUTES

The flavors of a fillet of grilled trout often depend on the type of water they lived in: The ideal water is cold as the fish will taste very fresh and tender. Lake trout will be a little less tender but still flavorful. Garlic and herbs enhance the flavors of the trout.

Garlic and Herbs

1 Add the olive oil to a small saucepan over medium-high heat. When hot, stir in the garlic and cook until golden, about 2 minutes. Stir in the white wine vinegar, lemon juice, rosemary, sage, and thyme into a small bowl and simmer for 1 minute. Remove and let infuse for 30 minutes.

2 Place the trout fillets to a large baking dish and cover with the garlic and herb oil; if the mixture doesn't cover the fillets, make note and flip halfway during marinating. Transfer the dish to the refrigerator and let the fillets rest in the oil for 30 to 45 minutes.

3 Prepare your gas or charcoal grill to medium-high heat.

4 When the grill is ready, at about 400 to 500 degrees with the coals lightly covered with ash, remove the fillets from the garlic and herb marinade and season with coarsely ground black pepper and sea salt. Place the fillets on the grill, skin-side down, and cook for about 2 to 3 minutes per side. Transfer the fillets from the grill to a large carving board and let rest for 10 minutes. Serve warm.

INGREDIENTS

½ cup olive oil

4 garlic cloves, finely chopped

2 tablespoons white wine vinegar

¼ small lemon, juiced

2 teaspoons fresh rosemary

1 teaspoon fresh sage

½ teaspoon fresh thyme

8 trout fillets, about 2 pounds

Coarsely ground black pepper

Fresh sea salt

Spiced-Honey Salmon

MAKES 4 SERVINGS • ACTIVE TIME: 25 MINUTES
TOTAL TIME: 1 HOUR AND 10 MINUTES

The sweet flavor of the honey pairs well with the fresh flavors of the salmon. Serve with asparagus.

1 Combine the honey, chives, hot water, garlic clove, and lemon juice in a small food processor and blend to a paste. Remove the paste from the processor and coat the fillets evenly with the mixture. Season with coarsely ground black pepper and fresh sea salt. Set aside and let marinate for at least 30 minutes.

2 Preheat your gas or charcoal grill to medium-high heat.

3 When the grill is ready, at about 450 to 500 degrees with the coals lightly covered with ash, place the salmon fillets over direct heat and cook for about 4 minutes per side, until the fish is flakey when pierced with a fork.

4 Transfer the honey-glazed fillets to a cutting board and let rest for 5 to 10 minutes before serving.

TOOLS

Food processor

INGREDIENTS

4 tablespoons honey

1 tablespoon fresh chives, chopped

2 teaspoons hot water

1 large garlic clove, peeled

½ small lemon, juiced

4 salmon fillets, about 4-inch squares

Coarsely ground black pepper

Fresh sea salt

Sauces

Sauces, gravies, and glazes make whatever meat is on your grill a memorable meal. With the recipes in this chapter, you'll discover there's a simple framework for making sauces and gravies. Add the right ingredients at the right times, and you'll have a sauce perfect for whatever you're grilling.

Sauces are structured with one of two foundational components: liquids or vegetables. Nearly all sauces that are liquids start with oil, cream, stock, broth, beer, wine, or liquor.

Sauces made from vegetables, such as a chimichurri or basil pesto, don't take long to prepare, and they're compatible with a variety of meats. Ingredients for these sauces are typically either finely chopped and then combined in a small bowl with some extra-virgin olive oil, or pulsed in a food processor with the olive oil gradually beat in.

For any sort of gravy, a roux is a necessary component. A white roux is composed of equal parts butter and flour and can either be made ahead of time or added to the sauce toward the end of the cooking process. When making ahead, set a small frying pan over medium heat and add 1 or 2 tablespoons of unsalted butter to the pan. When it has melted, stir in an equal amount of flour and beat into the butter until the roux reaches a thick mixture. The roux should not be browned, though it should have a hint of gold. Add the white roux toward the end of the sauce's cooking and then continue to heat for another 1 to 2 minutes so the sauce thickens and becomes a gravy.

Au Jus

Au Jus, literally meaning "with its own juices," is the classic accompaniment to all prime rib dinners. At its most basic form, au jus is a combination of the cooked proteins found in the muscles and fibers from the meat, along with the lipids from the blood. Since these "juices" of the meat come naturally with a slow-roasting technique (note that some sort of roasting pan is required to catch the juices), they serve as the most foundational element to any sauce or gravy that you prepare for your dinner. Because the earthy, natural flavors of a classic au jus are extremely compatible and accessible, they pair well with practically all elements of the dinner.

To begin, remove the rib roast from the pan and strain the pan drippings through a fine sieve. Then, pass the strained juiced through a fat separator (a simple spoon will do). For more flavor, do not discard the browned bits that have remained on the bottom of the roasting pan. Add the juices to the roasting pan and set over medium-high heat; note that you may need to use two burners.

Now it's time to add fundamental elements to your au jus that will enhance its consistency and flavor. For a rib roast, you'll want to find a nice bottle of dry red wine—preferably the same one that you'll be serving with dinner—and add 1 cup of it to your roasting pan, along with 2 cups of beef broth (note the 1:2 ratio here between the red wine and beef broth). Do not add a stock to your au jus; always a broth. A beef stock will actually have too much flavor and it will overpower your au jus.

With the roasting pan placed over medium-high heat, bring your juices to a boil and then reduce until you have about 1 to 1$\frac{1}{2}$ cups of au jus. Stir the au jus occasionally, scraping off the browned bits from the bottom so that they naturally are incorporated into the au jus.

Finally, you'll need to add seasonings to your au jus. Depending on the environment and mood of your dinner, you may want to pair the rib roast with the most natural form of au jus. If this is the case, you'll want to remove the roasting pan from the heat and season with the coarsely ground black pepper and fresh sea salt. However, if you want to add some additional natural ingredients to your au jus, consider a couple tablespoons of finely chopped fresh herbs such as thyme, rosemary, or flat-leaf parsley. If you want a little creaminess, whisk in 1 tablespoon of unsalted butter just before seasoning with the coarsely ground black pepper and fresh sea salt. Some chefs will even add soy sauce or Worcestershire sauce to the au jus at this final stage, and I encourage you to try that once in a while.

Although the classic au jus is most often imagined alongside a rib roast, it is essential to understand that an au jus can really be prepared with any slow-roasted meat, including poultry. For your convenience, I've prepared three basic ingredient lists for au jus, including one for poultry dishes, so that you can see the flexibility of an au jus and hopefully get an idea of where and how you'll want to experiment. Follow the three stages listed above and you'll have your very own au jus in no time at all.

Basic Au Jus

1 cup dry red wine

2 cups beef broth

1 tablespoon unsalted
butter (optional)

Coarsely ground
black pepper

Fresh sea salt

TIP: AU JUS INSTRUCTIONS
ARE ON PAGES 226 AND 227.

Au Jus with Herbs

1 cup dry red wine

2 cups beef broth

1 teaspoon fresh
rosemary, finely
chopped

1 teaspoon fresh
thyme, finely chopped

1 teaspoon flat-leaf
parsley, finely chopped

1 teaspoon Worcestershire
sauce (optional)

Coarsely ground
black pepper

Fresh sea salt

Poultry Au Jus

1 cup dry white wine

2 cups chicken broth

2 teaspoons flat-leaf
parsley, finely chopped

1 tablespoon
unsalted butter

Coarsely ground
black pepper

Fresh sea salt

Prime Rib Gravy

MAKES 6 TO 8 SERVINGS · ACTIVE TIME: 20 MINUTES · TOTAL TIME: 30 MINUTES

WORKS BEST WITH: ☑ **RED MEAT** ☐ **PORK** ☐ **POULTRY** ☑ **SEAFOOD**

FLAVOR: ☐ **SPICY** ☐ **SWEET** ☐ **TANGY** ☑ **SAVORY** ☐ **SALTY**

CONSISTENCY: ☐ **COARSE** ☑ **COATING** ☑ **POURING**

The fundamental part to any gravy comes from the juices leftover in the pan after the rib roast has been cooked. Likewise, your gravy goes hand-in-hand with the roasting technique—it's essential that you use a technique that involves a roasting pan so that the juices from the prime rib slowly accumulate at the bottom of the pan.

A gravy is not too different from an au jus, other than that it adds a white roux to the cooking process. As a reminder, a white roux is comprised of equal parts flour and butter and is usually added to a sauce to serve as a natural thickener, creating a gravy.

1 When the roast is finished, remove it and the roasting rack from the pan and transfer to a large carving board. Cover the roast with a sheet or two of aluminum foil so it stays warm. Pour the juices from the roasting pan into a fat separator; discard the fat and return the juices to the original roasting pan. Note that there is still flavor blanketing the roasting pan, so be sure to use the same pan.

2 Set the roasting pan over high heat—it may be necessary to use two burners if the roasting rack is too large for one. Add the red wine and stock or broth to the pan and bring to a light simmer, using a wooden spatula to scrape off any bits that still remain on the bottom of the pan so they are incorporated into the sauce.

3 Whisk the butter into the sauce, followed by the flour. Depending on how thick you want the gravy, add more butter and flour in incremental, equal proportions.

4 When thickened, about 1 to 2 minutes later, turn the heat off and stir in the thyme. Taste the gravy and season with the coarsely ground black pepper and fresh sea salt; then transfer to a small gravy boat. Serve hot.

INGREDIENTS

1 cup dry red wine

1½ cups beef or veal stock or broth

1 tablespoon unsalted butter

1 tablespoon all-purpose flour

1 tablespoon fresh thyme, finely chopped

Coarsely ground black pepper

Fresh sea salt

TIP: IF YOU DON'T HAVE A FAT SEPARATOR, BRING THE ROASTING PAN TO THE SINK AND TILT TO ONE SIDE. NEXT, WITH A LARGE SPOON OR LADLE, SLOWLY SPOON AWAY THE FAT THAT REMAINS AT THE TOP OF THE DISH.

Madeira Sauce

MAKES 6 SERVINGS • **ACTIVE TIME: 20 MINUTES** • **TOTAL TIME: 25 MINUTES**

WORKS BEST WITH: ☑ RED MEAT ☑ PORK ☐ POULTRY ☐ SEAFOOD

FLAVOR: ☐ SPICY ☑ SWEET ☐ TANGY ☑ SAVORY ☑ SALTY

CONSISTENCY: ☐ COARSE ☑ COATING ☑ POURING

At the White Barn Inn in Kennebunk, Maine, where I worked for some time, we always paired a classic Madeira sauce with our beef tenderloin, served over whipped potatoes. A very condensed sauce, the most fundamental element to a Madeira is the beef stock. Fresh beef stock is always best. Chances are, your local butcher can give you either a fresh stock or the best instructions on how use their bones properly in your stock.

1 Add the butter to a medium cast-iron skillet and warm over medium heat. Then add the chopped shallot and sauté until translucent, about 4 minutes.

2 Add the flour to the pan and cook for 1 minute. Once incorporated, turn the heat to medium-low and then add the dry red wine, Madeira, beef stock or broth, thyme, and rosemary.

3 Cook until the sauce has been significantly reduced, to your desired consistency, about 15 to 20 minutes.

When the sauce is reduced, remove the skillet from the stovetop and season with the coarsely ground black pepper and fresh sea salt. Spoon the Madeira sauce over the cuts of rib roast.

VARIATION: If you want a stronger Madeira sauce, add 1 tablespoon of beef demi-glace to the sauce along with the beef stock. You can find beef demi-glace at the grocery store near the beef broths and stocks.

INGREDIENTS

2 tablespoons unsalted butter

1 small shallot, finely chopped

1 tablespoon all-purpose flour

¼ cup dry red wine

¾ cup Madeira

1 cup beef stock or broth, canned or purchased from local butcher

2 sprigs fresh thyme, leaves removed

2 sprigs fresh rosemary, leaves removed

Coarsely ground black pepper

Fresh sea salt

Homemade Ketchup

MAKES 6 SERVINGS • **ACTIVE TIME: 20 MINUTES** • **TOTAL TIME: 25 MINUTES**

WORKS BEST WITH:	☑ RED MEAT	☐ PORK	☑ POULTRY	☐ SEAFOOD
FLAVOR:	☑ SPICY	☐ SWEET	☑ TANGY	☐ SAVORY	☑ SALTY
CONSISTENCY:	☑ COARSE	☐ COATING	☐ POURING

Most ketchup made by large-scale manufacturers is largely based in sucrose. Because of this, when we have natural, homemade ketchup, we tend to think of it as something entirely different than ketchup. Homemade ketchup should always be grounded in puréed tomatoes and vinegar.

1 In a medium bowl, combine the puréed tomatoes, lemon juice, extra-virgin olive oil, onion, garlic, and dark brown sugar. Let rest for 15 minutes.

2 Gradually whisk in the apple cider vinegar and water. Season with the coarsely ground black pepper and fresh sea salt.

3 You can serve your ketchup right away or let the flavors meld overnight in the refrigerator.

INGREDIENTS

3 cups puréed tomatoes

¼ medium lemon, juiced

2 tablespoons extra-virgin olive oil

½ medium white onion, finely chopped

2 garlic cloves, minced

¼ cup dark brown sugar

½ cup apple cider vinegar

½ cup water

Coarsely ground black pepper

Fresh sea salt

Pizzaiola Sauce

...KES 6 TO 8 SERVINGS • ACTIVE TIME: 35 MINUTES • TOTAL TIME: 45 MINUTES

...KS BEST WITH: ☑ RED MEAT ☑ PORK ☑ POULTRY ☐ SEAFOOD

...VOR: ☐ SPICY ☐ SWEET ☐ TANGY ☑ SAVORY ☑ SALTY

...NSISTENCY: ☑ COARSE ☐ COATING ☐ POURING

...rst had a version of this dish at The Palm Restaurant in New York ...y. My father and I ordered two New York strips and then, rather ...expectedly, a side of spicy marinara, just slightly less complex ...n a pizzaiola sauce. With the beef and pizzaiola combined, the ...vors were simply breathtaking—spicy though sweet; rich yet light. ...eks later, I tried this pizzaiola sauce with a rotisserie-style rib ...st and the flavors exploded—there's really nothing quite like ...izzaiola!

1 Put the extra-virgin olive oil in a cast-iron skillet and place over medium heat. When the oil is hot, add the garlic and cook until golden, about 1 to 2 minutes.

2 Add the plum tomatoes, sun-dried tomatoes, oregano, thyme, and red pepper flakes if using. Simmer for 15 minutes, and then add the wine and basil and season with pepper and salt.

3 Simmer for 20 more minutes, then remove the skillet from the stovetop and serve warm.

INGREDIENTS

¼ cup extra-virgin olive oil

4 garlic cloves, finely chopped

2 pounds plum tomatoes, crushed by hand

¼ cup sun-dried tomatoes

1 sprig fresh oregano

1 sprig fresh thyme

1 teaspoon red pepper flakes (optional)

¼ cup dry white wine

½ cup fresh basil leaves, finely chopped

Coarsely ground black pepper

Fresh sea salt

Smoked Southern

MAKES 6 TO 8 SERVINGS • ACTIVE TIME: 35 MINUTES • TOTAL TIME: 55 MINUTES

WORKS BEST WITH:	☑ RED MEAT	☑ PORK	☑ POULTRY	☐ SEAFOOD
FLAVOR:	☑ SPICY	☐ SWEET	☐ TANGY	☑ SAVORY ☑ SALTY
CONSISTENCY:	☐ COARSE	☑ COATING	☐ POURING	

This sauce is filled with intense spice and goes great when served on or alongside barbecued beef and pork dishes, such as smoked brisket (pages 87 and 88) or baby back ribs (page 374).

TOOLS

2 to 3 cups hickory or oak woodchips

INGREDIENTS

2 garlic cloves, finely chopped

1 medium white onion, finely chopped

1½ cups canned crushed tomatoes

½ cup tomato paste

¼ cup white wine vinegar

¼ cup balsamic vinegar

2 tablespoons Dijon mustard

1 medium lime, juiced

2 tablespoons ginger, finely chopped

1 teaspoon smoked paprika

½ teaspoon ground cinnamon

2 dried chipotle peppers, finely chopped

1 habanero pepper, seeded and finely chopped (optional)

1 cup water

Coarsely ground black pepper

Fresh sea salt

BBQ Sauce

1 An hour before grilling, add the woodchips into a bowl of water and let soak.

2 Prepare your gas or charcoal grill to medium-high heat.

3 While waiting for the grill to heat up, place a small frying pan over medium heat and, when hot, add the garlic and onion and cook until the garlic has browned and the onion is translucent. Remove and set aside.

4 Transfer the cooked garlic and onion into a food processor, followed by the tomatoes and tomato paste. Purée into a thick paste, and then add the remaining ingredients to the food processor and blend thorough. Transfer the sauce into a medium saucepan and set it near the grill.

5 When the grill is ready, about 400 to 450 degrees with the coals lightly covered with ash, drain 1 cup of the woodchips and spread over the coals or pour in the smoker box. Place the medium saucepan on the grill and then bring the sauce to a boil with the grill's lid covered, aligning the air vent away from the woodchips so that their smoke rolls around the sauce before escaping. Let the sauce cook for about 30 to 45 minutes, every 20 minutes adding another cup of drained woodchips, until it has reduced to about 2 cups.

6 Remove the sauce from the heat and serve warm. The sauce can be kept refrigerated for up to 2 weeks.

> **TIP:** OMIT THE HABANERO PEPPER IF YOU DON'T LIKE YOUR BARBECUE SAUCE AS HOT.

Maple BBQ Sauce

MAKES 6 TO 8 SERVINGS • ACTIVE TIME: 10 MINUTES • TOTAL TIME: 25 MINUTES

WORKS BEST WITH:	☑ RED MEAT	☑ PORK	☑ POULTRY	☐ SEAFOOD
FLAVOR:	☑ SPICY	☑ SWEET	☐ TANGY	☑ SAVORY	☐ SALTY
CONSISTENCY:	☐ COARSE	☑ COATING	☐ POURING

The maple flavor that comes from the maple syrup works so well with all pork recipes. Try this recipe as a basting sauce for pork ribs.

INGREDIENTS

¼ small white onion, finely chopped

2 garlic cloves, minced

1 cup ketchup

3 tablespoons apple cider vinegar

1 tablespoon clarified butter

½ cup organic maple syrup

2 tablespoons organic molasses

2 teaspoons ground mustard

Coarsely ground black pepper

Fresh sea salt

1 Place a medium saucepan over medium-high heat. When hot, add in the onion and garlic and cook until the onion is translucent and the garlic is golden, not brown—about 1 to 2 minutes.

2 Add in the remaining ingredients and bring to a boil.

3 Reduce the sauce to a simmer and then cook, uncovered, for about 20 minutes.

4 When the sauce has reduced to about 1 to 2 cups, remove from heat and refrigerate for an hour before serving.

Apple-Mustard BBQ Sauce

MAKES 6 TO 8 SERVINGS

WORKS BEST WITH:	☐ RED MEAT	☑ PORK	☑ POULTRY	☐ SEAFOOD
FLAVOR: ☐ SPICY	☑ SWEET	☐ TANGY	☑ SAVORY	☐ SALTY
CONSISTENCY: ☐ COARSE	☑ COATING	☑ POURING		

This smoky sauce goes well with poultry, pork, and lamb dishes and should be generously applied to the meat.

Combine all the ingredients into a small bowl and refrigerate for 1 hour before applying to the meat.

TIP: USE THIS SAUCE FOR RIBS!

INGREDIENTS

1 tablespoon olive oil

¼ small shallot, finely chopped

¼ cup apple cider

¼ cup white wine vinegar

1 tablespoon tequila

2 teaspoon fresh parsley, finely chopped

3 tablespoons fresh fish sauce

1 tablespoon raw honey

1 tablespoon Dijon mustard

2 teaspoons hot Chinese mustard

Coarsely ground black pepper

Basil Pesto

MAKES 6 SERVINGS • ACTIVE TIME: 15 MINUTES • TOTAL TIME: 15 MINUTES

WORKS BEST WITH:	☑ RED MEAT	☑ PORK	☑ POULTRY	☑ SEAFOOD
FLAVOR:	☐ SPICY	☐ SWEET	☐ TANGY	☑ SAVORY	☐ SALTY
CONSISTENCY:	☑ COARSE	☑ COATING	☐ POURING

Pesto is rooted in herbs and pine nuts—two of the most versatile flavors. Use this on pasta as a sauce, as a crust for a rib roast, or as a topping on a baked potato.

1 Add 2 teaspoons of the extra-virgin olive oil to a small frying pan and place on the stovetop over medium heat. When hot, add the pine nuts and toast for a minute or two until golden, not browned. Remove from the heat and transfer to a small cup.

2 In a small food processor, pulse the pine nuts, basil leaves, shallot, and garlic into a thick paste. Next, slowly incorporate the remaining extra-virgin olive oil into the pesto, until you reach your desired consistency.

3 Using a spatula, remove the pesto from the processor and place in a medium bowl. With a spoon, mix in the Parmesan cheese and then season with the coarsely ground black pepper and fresh sea salt. Serve at room temperature, or lightly chilled.

VARIATION: If you want a coarser pesto (or don't have a food processor), you can always use a chef's knife and cutting board to chop the ingredients. In a small bowl, combine them, and then let the pesto marinate for 1 hour before serving.

INGREDIENTS

⅓ cup, plus
2 teaspoons
extra-virgin
olive oil

⅓ cup pine nuts

3 cups fresh
basil leaves

¼ small shallot

2 garlic cloves

¼ cup Parmesan
cheese, freshly grated

Coarsely ground
black pepper

Fresh sea salt

Sun-Dried Tomato Pesto

MAKES 6 TO 8 SERVINGS • ACTIVE TIME: 10 MINUTES • TOTAL TIME: 15 MINUTES

WORKS BEST WITH:	☑ RED MEAT	☑ PORK	☑ POULTRY	☑ SEAFOOD
FLAVOR:	☐ SPICY	☐ SWEET	☐ TANGY	☑ SAVORY	☐ SALTY
CONSISTENCY:	☑ COARSE	☑ COATING	☐ POURING	

This is such an easy recipe to make—all you need is a food processor, or just a chef's knife, a carving board, and a small bowl to hold everything!

INGREDIENTS

12 sun-dried tomatoes

½ cup fresh basil leaves

¼ small shallot

¼ cup pine nuts

1 garlic clove

1 tablespoon coarsely ground black pepper

1 teaspoon fresh sea salt

½ cup extra-virgin olive oil

1 In a small food processor, combine all the ingredients except the extra-virgin olive oil and pulse into a thick mixture.

2 Slowly add the extra-virgin olive oil and process until reaching your desired consistency. Serve at room temperature or lightly chilled.

VARIATION: If you want a coarser pesto (or don't have a food processor), you can always use a chef's knife and cutting board to chop the ingredients. In a small bowl, combine them, and then let the pesto marinate for 1 hour before serving.

> **TIP:** SERVE SUN-DRIED TOMATO PESTO ALONGSIDE GRILLED STEAKS.

Garlic and Chive Steak Sauce

WORKS BEST WITH: ☑ RED MEAT ☐ PORK ☑ POULTRY ☑ SEAFOOD

FLAVOR: ☑ SPICY ☐ SWEET ☑ TANGY ☐ SAVORY ☐ SALTY

1 In a small bowl, whisk together the sour cream, chives, garlic, and lemon juice, and then season the sauce with coarsely ground black pepper.

2 Store in the refrigerator for up to 3 days, and serve at room temperature.

> THE FLAVOR OF CHIVES IS VERY SIMILAR TO THAT OF A MILD ONION.

INGREDIENTS

½ cup sour cream

¼ cup fresh chives, finely chopped

3 garlic cloves, minced

¼ small lemon, juiced

Coarsely ground black pepper

Fresh sea salt

Kansas City BBQ Sauce

MAKES 5 CUPS • **ACTIVE TIME: 15 MINUTES** • **TOTAL TIME: 40 MINUTES**

WORKS BEST WITH: ☑ RED MEAT ☑ PORK ☑ POULTRY ☑ SEAFOOD

FLAVOR: ☐ SPICY ☐ SWEET ☐ TANGY ☑ SAVORY ☐ SALTY

CONSISTENCY: ☑ COARSE ☑ COATING ☐ POURING

1 Heat the olive oil in a saucepan over medium heat. Add the minced garlic cloves and cook until golden, about 2 minutes.

2 Mix the remaining ingredients into the saucepan and bring to a simmer. Then cover the saucepan and cook until the sauce has been reduced by half, roughly 25 minutes. Make sure to mix the sauce occasionally.

3 When the sauce has been reduced by half, remove from heat, discard bay leaf, and let rest for 10 minutes before serving.

VARIATION: For more of a kick, try adding half of a finely chopped habanero pepper. Be careful, though, the more seeds you add the hotter it will become!

INGREDIENTS

2 tablespoons olive oil

4 garlic cloves, minced

2 cups ketchup

1 cup water

¼ cup molasses

¼ cup dark brown sugar

¼ cup apple cider vinegar

2 tablespoons Worcestershire sauce

1 bay leaf

1 teaspoon mustard powder

1 teaspoon chili powder

1 teaspoon onion powder

2 teaspoons liquid smoke

1 teaspoon ground black pepper

1 teaspoon sea salt

South Carolina Mustard BBQ Sauce

MAKES 2 CUPS • **ACTIVE TIME: 10 MINUTES** • **TOTAL TIME: 1 HOUR**

WORKS BEST WITH: ☑ RED MEAT ☑ PORK ☑ POULTRY ☑ SEAFOOD

FLAVOR: ☐ SPICY ☐ SWEET ☐ TANGY ☑ SAVORY ☐ SALTY

CONSISTENCY: ☑ COARSE ☑ COATING ☐ POURING

INGREDIENTS

¾ cup yellow mustard

¼ cup honey

¼ cup apple cider vinegar

1 tablespoon ketchup

1 tablespoon light brown sugar

2 teaspoons Worcestershire sauce

3 garlic cloves, minced

1 teaspoon ground black pepper

In a bowl, combine all of the ingredients and let rest for 1 hour in the refrigerator before serving.

Spicy Peach BBQ Sauce

MAKES 4 CUPS • **ACTIVE TIME: 15 MINUTES** • **TOTAL TIME: 30 MINUTES**

WORKS BEST WITH:	☑ RED MEAT	☐ PORK	☑ POULTRY	☑ SEAFOOD
FLAVOR:	☑ SPICY	☐ SWEET	☑ TANGY	☐ SAVORY	☐ SALTY
CONSISTENCY:	☑ COARSE	☑ COATING	POURING	

1 Heat the olive oil in a saucepan over medium heat. Add the minced garlic and onion to the saucepan, and cook until golden, about 2 minutes.

2 Mix the remaining ingredients into the saucepan, bring to a simmer, and then cover the saucepan and cook until the sauce has been reduced by half, roughly 10 to 15 minutes. Stir occasionally while sauce is covered.

3 When the sauce has been reduced, remove from heat and let rest for 10 minutes before serving.

INGREDIENTS

2 tablespoons olive oil

4 garlic cloves, minced

1 small onion, finely chopped

1 cup pureed tomatoes

½ cup ketchup

¼ cup light brown sugar

¼ cup molasses

2 tablespoons honey

1 tablespoon Worcestershire sauce

4 peaches, peeled, cored, and chopped

2 tablespoon peach preserves

½ small lemon, juiced

1 teaspoon ground black pepper

1 teaspoon sea salt

St. Louis BBQ Sauce

MAKES 4 TO 5 CUPS • ACTIVE TIME: 20 MINUTES • TOTAL TIME: 1 HOUR 15 MINUTES

WORKS BEST WITH: ☑ RED MEAT ☑ PORK ☑ POULTRY ☑ SEAFOOD

FLAVOR: ☐ SPICY ☐ SWEET ☐ TANGY ☑ SAVORY ☐ SALTY

CONSISTENCY: ☑ COARSE ☑ COATING ☐ POURING

INGREDIENTS

1 can pureed tomatoes

2 tablespoons Dijon mustard

¼ cup apple cider vinegar

¼ cup molasses

1 cup dark brown sugar

1 teaspoon Worcestershire sauce

2 garlic cloves, minced

1 teaspoon ground black pepper

1 teaspoon sea salt

1 Combine all ingredients in a saucepan and place over medium-high heat. Bring the sauce to a boil, cover, and let cook—continuing to boil—for 6 minutes.

2 Reduce the heat to low, and cook for about 1 hour, stirring occasionally, until the sauce has thickened and reduced by half.

3 Remove from heat and let stand for 10 minutes before serving.

Honey Bourbon BBQ Sauce

MAKES 3 CUPS • **ACTIVE TIME: 8 MINUTES** • **TOTAL TIME: 20 MINUTES**

WORKS BEST WITH: ☑ RED MEAT ☑ PORK ☑ POULTRY ☑ SEAFOOD

FLAVOR: ☐ SPICY ☐ SWEET ☐ TANGY ☑ SAVORY ☐ SALTY

CONSISTENCY: ☑ COARSE ☑ COATING ☐ POURING

INGREDIENTS

2 tablespoons olive oil

4 garlic cloves, minced

1 cup ketchup

½ cup bourbon

3 tablespoons honey

2 tablespoons brown sugar

1 tablespoon soy sauce

1 tablespoon Worcestershire sauce

1 tablespoon Dijon mustard

1 teaspoon liquid smoke

1 teaspoon ground black pepper

1 teaspoon sea salt

1 Heat the olive oil in a saucepan over medium heat. Add the minced garlic cloves, and cook until golden, about 2 minutes.

2 Next, stir in the remaining ingredients and bring to a boil. Reduce the heat immediately, cover, and cook for about 6 minutes, until the sauce has reduced by about half.

3 Remove from heat, let stand for 10 minutes, and serve.

Miso BBQ Sauce

MAKES 2 CUPS • **ACTIVE TIME: 5 MINUTES** • **TOTAL TIME: 5 MINUTES**

WORKS BEST WITH: ☑ RED MEAT ☐ PORK ☑ POULTRY ☑ SEAFOOD

FLAVOR: ☑ SPICY ☐ SWEET ☑ TANGY ☐ SAVORY ☐ SALTY

CONSISTENCY: ☑ COARSE ☑ COATING ☐ POURING

In a bowl, use a fork to combine all of the ingredients and stir until the desired consistency has been reached.

INGREDIENTS

3 tablespoons red or white miso

2 tablespoons water

2 garlic cloves, minced

3 tablespoons dark brown sugar

3 tablespoons white vinegar

2 tablespoons ketchup

1 teaspoon ground black pepper

1 teaspoon sea salt

Korean BBQ Sauce

MAKES 3 CUPS • **ACTIVE TIME: 15 MINUTES** • **TOTAL TIME: 35 MINUTES**

WORKS BEST WITH: ☑ RED MEAT ☑ PORK ☑ POULTRY ☑ SEAFOOD

FLAVOR: ☐ SPICY ☐ SWEET ☐ TANGY ☑ SAVORY ☐ SALTY

CONSISTENCY: ☑ COARSE ☑ COATING ☐ POURING

INGREDIENTS

½ cup soy sauce

¼ cup ketchup

¼ cup rice wine vinegar

3 tablespoons light brown sugar

1 teaspoon gochujang (red chili paste)

2 garlic cloves, minced

1 teaspoon sesame oil

1 teaspoon fresh ginger, grated

4 scallions, chopped

1 teaspoon ground black pepper

1 Place a small saucepan over medium heat.

2 Add the soy sauce, ketchup, rice wine vinegar, light brown sugar, gochujang, and minced garlic into the saucepan, and stir until thoroughly combined. Bring to a simmer, cover the saucepan, and let simmer for 15 to 20 minutes, until the sauce has reduced by half.

3 Stir in the remaining ingredients, cook for 2 more minutes, and remove from heat.

4 Let the sauce stand for 10 minutes before serving.

Smoky BBQ Beer Sauce

MAKES 4 CUPS • **ACTIVE TIME: 15 MINUTES** • **TOTAL TIME: 30 MINUTES**

WORKS BEST WITH: ☑ RED MEAT ☑ PORK ☑ POULTRY ☑ SEAFOOD

FLAVOR: ☐ SPICY ☐ SWEET ☐ TANGY ☑ SAVORY ☐ SALTY

CONSISTENCY: ☑ COARSE ☑ COATING ☐ POURING

INGREDIENTS

1 cup stout beer

1 cup ketchup

½ cup apple cider vinegar

½ cup dark brown sugar

2 tablespoons honey

2 tablespoons Worcestershire sauce

1 teaspoon liquid smoke

1 teaspoon coarsely ground black pepper

1 teaspoon sea salt

1 Place a small saucepan over medium heat and add all of the ingredients to the saucepan. Bring to a boil, reduce heat, and let simmer for roughly 20 minutes until the sauce has reduced by a third.

2 Remove from heat and let stand for 10 minutes before serving.

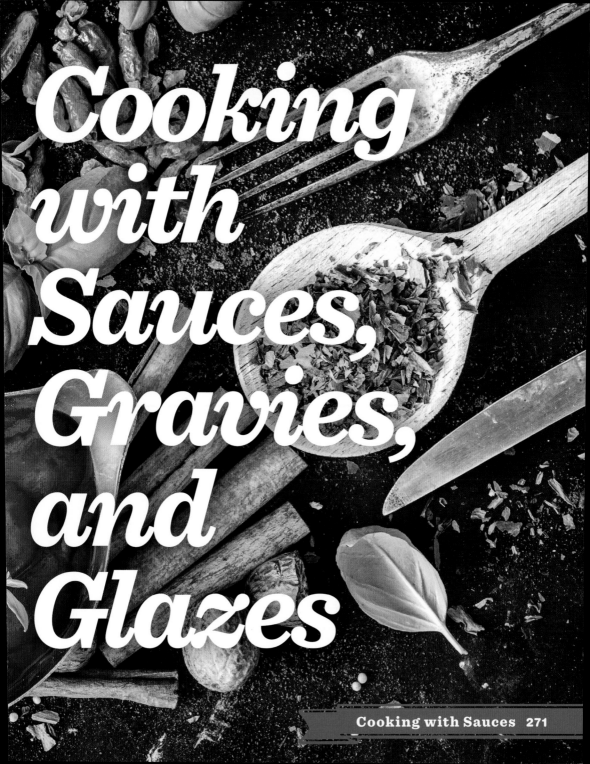

Cooking with Sauces, Gravies, and Glazes

Onion-and-Garlic

MAKES 4 TO 6 SERVINGS • ACTIVE TIME: 30 MINUTES
TOTAL TIME: 1 HOUR AND 10 MINUTES

Mussels are great when flavored with some lemon and garlic. You can also pop them in a seafood stew (page 274).

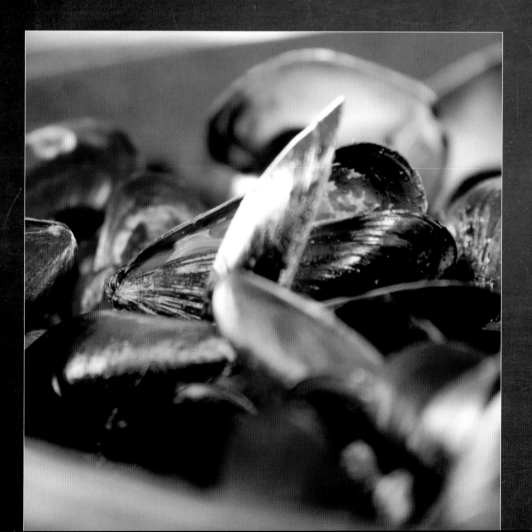

Smoked Mussels

1 In a large bowl, combine the cleaned mussels, parsley, 4 of the minced garlic cloves, and olive oil and toss evenly. Next, squeeze the lemon halves over the mussels and then season with coarsely ground black pepper and sea salt.

2 An hour before grilling, add the yellow onion and 4 remaining minced garlic cloves into a bowl of warm water; let soak.

3 Preheat your gas or charcoal grill to medium-high heat.

4 When the grill is ready, at about 450 to 500 degrees with the coals lightly covered with ash, toss the soaked onion and garlic cloves over the coals, or into the smoking box. Wait 5 minutes for the smoke to develop (there will not be as much smoke as from traditional woodchips). Add the mussels to a grill basket (or a sheet of aluminum foil will do) and place on the grill. Cover the grill and cook for about 10 minutes until the mussels are opened.

5 Remove mussels when opened; for ones that haven't opened, try cooking them a bit longer and throw them out if they don't open. Transfer the mussels to a large bowl and let rest, uncovered, for 5 to 10 minutes before serving.

INGREDIENTS

2 to 3 pounds mussels, cleaned and debearded

4 tablespoons fresh flat-leaf parsley, chopped

8 garlic cloves, 4 minced

4 tablespoons olive oil

1 lemon, halved

Coarsely ground black pepper

Fresh sea salt

1 medium yellow onion, quartered

Grilled Seafood Stew

MAKES 4 TO 6 SERVINGS • ACTIVE TIME: 45 MINUTES • TOTAL TIME: 1 HOUR

Always a favorite amongst seafood lovers, this classic dish tastes best when served in a tomato broth. Serve in large bowls and, if you would like, garnish with finely chopped, fresh flat-leaf parsley leaves. Place a bowl to the side for empty shells.

INGREDIENTS

¼ cup olive oil

1 large shallot, finely chopped

4 garlic cloves, minced

¼ small green pepper, chopped

½ teaspoon dried oregano

½ teaspoon red pepper flakes

3 cups plum tomatoes, stemmed and crushed

2 tablespoons flat-leaf parsley, leaves removed

2 thyme sprigs

1 bay leaf

½ small lemon, juiced

2 cups clam juice

1 cup dry white wine

24 littleneck clams, scrubbed

18 mussels, scrubbed

14 large shrimp, peeled and deveined

10 2x1-inch pieces of striped bass

Coarsely ground black pepper

Fresh sea salt

in Tomato Broth

1 Place a large Dutch oven on your gas or charcoal grill and prepare to medium-high heat. Leave the grill covered while heating, as it will add a faint smoky flavor to the skillet.

2 When the grill is ready, at about 450 to 500 degrees with the coals lightly covered with ash, heat the olive oil in the Dutch oven. Next, when the oil is hot, add in the shallot and minced garlic and cook for about 2 minutes, until the shallot is translucent and the garlic is golden, not brown. Add in the green pepper, oregano, and red pepper flakes and cook until soft, about 5 minutes.

3 Add the tomatoes, parsley, thyme, bay leaf, lemon juice, clam juice, and dry white wine and boil until thickened, about 15 minutes.

4 Stir in the clams, mussels, and shrimp and cook until the shells open and the shrimp is firm. Add the pieces of striped bass and cook for another 3 minutes until the striped bass is opaque through the middle.

5 Remove the Dutch oven from the heat and season with coarsely ground black pepper and salt. Serve in warmed bowls.

Filet Mignon with

MAKES 2 TO 3 SERVINGS • ACTIVE TIME: 30 MINUTES • TOTAL TIME: 2 HOURS

A red wine reduction is a perfect accompaniment to filet mignon. Prepare the reduction in a cast-iron skillet after it has been used for the filet; this simple choice will bring out the most flavor in the reduction.

TOOLS

Butcher's twine

Cast-iron skillet

STEAK INGREDIENTS

2 filet mignon steaks, about 2 to 2½ inches thick

3 tablespoons olive oil

Coarsely ground black pepper

Fresh sea salt

SAUCE INGREDIENTS

2 tablespoons olive oil

½ shallot, finely chopped

1 tablespoon garlic, minced

1 teaspoon fresh oregano, finely chopped

1 cup Port wine

1 cup dry white wine

3 tablespoons balsamic vinegar

¼ cup fresh parsley, finely chopped

Coarsely ground black pepper

Fresh sea salt

Red Wine Reduction

1 Tie the butcher's string tightly around each steak. Then, rub both sides of the steaks with 2 tablespoons of the olive oil and let rest at room temperature for about 1 hour.

2 A half hour before cooking, place the cast-iron skillet on the grate and prepare your gas or charcoal grill to medium-high heat. Leave the grill covered while heating, as it will add a faint smoky flavor to the skillet.

3 When the grill is ready, at about 400 degrees with the coals lightly covered with ash, season one side of the steaks with half of the coarsely ground pepper and sea salt.

4 Spread the remaining tablespoon of olive oil in the skillet, and then place the steaks, seasoned sides down, into the cast-iron skillet. Wait 2 to 3 minutes until they are slightly charred, seasoning the uncooked sides of the steaks with the remaining pepper and sea salt while waiting. Flip the steaks and sear for another 2 to 3 minutes. Remove filets from the skillet and let rest, uncovered, for 30 minutes. Leave the skillet on the grill.

5 Preheat the oven to 400 degrees.

Continued on next page >

< Continued from previous page

6 While waiting for the oven, add the olive oil to the skillet and wait 30 seconds, scrapping the browned bits left by the filets from the bottom of the skillet. Stir in the shallots, garlic, and oregano and sauté for about 2 minutes, until tender and lightly browned. Add the Port, dry white wine, and balsamic vinegar and simmer until thickened and reduced by half. Add the parsley and simmer for 1 minute. Remove the skillet from heat and pour the reduction into a small bowl. Season with pepper and salt. Cover with aluminum foil and set aside.

7 Place the filets back into the cast-iron skillet and transfer to oven. For medium-rare, cook for 11 to 13 minutes or, for medium, for 14 to 15 minutes.

8 Remove the steaks from the oven and transfer to a large cutting board. Let stand for 10 minutes. Cut loose the butcher's string. Spoon the sauce over the filets and serve warm.

Skirt Steak with Olive Tapenade

MAKES 2 TO 3 SERVINGS • ACTIVE TIME: 30 MINUTES
TOTAL TIME: 1 HOUR AND 50 MINUTES

The skirt steak is often thought of as chewy. But that's only because it is thin and easy to overcook. Grill these steaks over direct heat and make sure not to cook past medium.

TAPENADE INGREDIENTS

1 cup Niçoise olives, pitted and chopped

½ cup olive oil

½ small shallot, minced

1 garlic clove, minced

1 sprig rosemary, leaves removed and finely minced

1 anchovy fillet (optional)

1 tablespoon fresh basil, finely chopped

1 tablespoon fresh flat-leaf parsley, finely chopped

1 tablespoon capers, minced

1 tablespoon fresh thyme

1 teaspoon red pepper flakes

STEAK INGREDIENTS

2 skirt steaks, about 1 to 1½ pounds each and ½ to ¾ inch thick

2 tablespoons olive oil

Coarsely ground black pepper

Fresh sea salt

Continued on next page >

< Continued from previous page

1 Rub both sides of the steaks with olive oil and let rest at room temperature for about 1 hour.

2 While waiting, combine the tapenade ingredients in a medium bowl and mix thoroughly. Set aside.

3 A half hour before cooking, prepare your gas or charcoal grill to extremely high heat.

4 When the grill is ready, about 500 to 600 degrees with the coals lightly covered with ash, season the steaks with the coarsely ground pepper and sea salt. Place the steaks on the grill and spoon a tablespoon or two of tapenade onto the top of each steak. Cook for about 3 minutes and then flip. Again, add a tablespoon of tapenade and cook for about 2 to 3 minutes for medium-rare, and 3 to 4 for medium. The steaks should be very charred and slightly firm if poked in the center.

5 Remove the steaks from the grill and transfer to a large cutting board. Let stand for 5 to 10 minutes. Slice the steak diagonally into long, thin slices and arrange the tapenade on the side. Serve warm.

Balsamic Glazed Flank Steak with Vidalia Onions and Mushrooms

Because of the balsamic glaze, the flank becomes much more tender than usual. This recipe includes Vidalia onions and mushrooms, which pair nicely with the balsamic glaze.

STEAK INGREDIENTS

1 flank steak, about 1 to 1½ pounds

2 tablespoons olive oil

Coarsely ground black pepper

Fresh sea salt

VIDALIA ONION & MUSHROOM INGREDIENTS

2 tablespoons olive oil

1½ pounds Vidalia onions, sliced to about ½ inch

1 pound mushrooms of your choice

GLAZE INGREDIENTS

1 cup balsamic vinegar

2 tablespoons clarified butter

1 sprig rosemary, leaves removed

Coarsely ground black pepper

Fresh sea salt

Continued on next page >

1 Rub the steak with olive oil and let rest at room temperature for about 1 hour.

2 A half hour before cooking, prepare your gas or charcoal grill to medium-high heat.

3 While waiting, prepare the Vidalia onions and mushrooms. Heat olive oil in a wide skillet over low heat. Add the onion slices and mushrooms and sear, stirring frequently, for 15 to 20 minutes until the onions are translucent and tender.

4 When the grill is ready, about 400 to 450 degrees and the coals are lightly covered with ash, season one side of the steak with half of the coarsely ground pepper and sea salt. Place the seasoned side of the steak on the grill and cook for about 4 to 5 minutes, seasoning the uncooked side of the steak while waiting. When the steak seems charred, gently flip and cook for 4 to 5 more minutes for medium-rare or 6 more minutes for medium. The steak should feel slightly firm if poked in the center.

5 Remove the steak from the grill and transfer to a large cutting board. Let stand for 6 to 8 minutes.

6 Add the balsamic vinegar to a small saucepan and bring to a boil over high-heat. Reduce to about 1/4 cup, about 6 to 7 minutes, and then stir in the clarified butter and rosemary. Remove from heat and season with pepper and salt.

7 Slice the steak diagonally into long, thin slices. Serve warm with the onions and mushrooms, and drizzle the balsamic glaze on top.

TIP: SLICE FLANK STEAK INTO VERY THIN STRIPS SO THAT IT'S NOT TOUGH.

Porterhouse Steak with

MAKES 2 TO 3 SERVINGS • **ACTIVE TIME: 35 MINUTES** • **TOTAL TIME: 2 HOURS**

Argentinian chimichurri sauce goes well with any steak. It can be used as marinade, though this is sometimes a little risky because of the light kick from the Fresno chile. I suggest serving the chimichurri sauce on the side, and for those who would like even more heat in the sauce, substitute a habanero in place of the Fresno chile!

Chimichurri Sauce

1 Rub both sides of the steaks with olive oil and let rest at room temperature for about 1 hour.

2 A half hour before cooking, prepare your gas or charcoal grill to medium-high heat.

3 While you wait, combine the vinegar, garlic, shallot, scallion, Fresno chile, lemon juice, and salt in a medium bowl and let rest for 15 minutes. Next, add the parsley, cilantro, and oregano, then gradually whisk in the olive oil. Set aside.

4 When the grill is ready, at about 400 to 450 degrees with the coals lightly covered with ash, season one side of the steaks with half of the coarsely ground pepper and sea salt, as well as a very light brush of the sauce along the bone.

5 Place the seasoned sides of the steaks on the grill and cook for about 5 to 6 minutes, seasoning the tops of the steaks while waiting. Again, lightly trace the bone with the sauce. When the steaks are charred, flip and cook for 4 to 5 more minutes for medium-rare or 6 to 7 minutes for medium. The steaks should feel slightly firm if poked in the center.

6 Remove the steaks from the grill and transfer to a large cutting board. Let stand for 10 minutes, allowing the steaks to properly store their juices and flavor. Serve warm with the chimichurri sauce on the side.

STEAK INGREDIENTS

2 porterhouse steaks, about 1½ inches thick

4 tablespoons olive oil

Coarsely ground black pepper

Fresh sea salt

SAUCE INGREDIENTS

½ cup red wine vinegar

4 garlic cloves, minced

1 shallot, minced

½ scallion, minced

1 Fresno chile, finely chopped (for additional spice, substitute in a minced habanero)

1 tablespoon fresh lemon juice

1 teaspoon fresh sea salt

½ cup fresh flat-leaf parsley, minced

½ cup fresh cilantro, minced

2 tablespoons fresh, minced oregano

¾ cup olive oil

Braised and Grilled Pork with Rosemary

MAKES 5 TO 6 SERVINGS • ACTIVE TIME: 45 MINUTES
TOTAL TIME: 1 HOUR AND 45 MINUTES

My favorite part about this dish is the way the rosemary needles catch and burn over the grill, bringing a charred and sweet flavor to the roast.

INGREDIENTS

2 sprigs rosemary (remove needles from their stems)

2¼ pounds boned pork loin

8 tablespoons olive oil

1 garlic clove, crushed

½ onion, chopped

¾ cup white wine

1 tablespoon white vinegar

Fresh sea salt

Coarsely ground black pepper

Continued on next page >

< Continued from previous page

1 To enhance the flavor and prevent the rosemary from searing completely off during the cooking process, push the rosemary needles into the pork loin. This will help infuse the flavor throughout the pork. Leave a little bit of each rosemary needle sticking out to catch and burn from the flame; this will add a lovely charred and sweet flavor to the roast.

2 Preheat your gas or charcoal grill to medium heat, and place a deep sauté pan on grilling rack so that it heats as well.

3 Brush and coat the roast with 1 tablespoon of the olive oil.

4 Place the roast into the deep sauté pan. Add the remaining oil into the pan, turning and cooking the pork evenly on all sides until it reaches a lovely golden brown.

5 Add the garlic, onion, remaining rosemary, wine, and vinegar and let the meat and seasoning cook together for about 1 hour. If you can control the temperature of your grill, bring the heat down so everything can simmer together for $1\frac{1}{2}$ hours.

6 Just before the pork appears to be done, remove it from the pan and place it directly on the grill to sear off the rosemary sprigs and gracefully char the exterior to your preference.

7 Remove the roast from the grill, and let it stand for 10 to 12 minutes. Slice thin before serving, and use some of the cooked juices as a light gravy if the pork happens to get slightly overdone.

VARIATION: Swap out the rosemary for 3 tablespoons freshly chopped dill.

Killer Barbeque Spare Ribs

**MAKES 6 TO 8 SERVINGS • ACTIVE TIME: 1 HOUR AND MINUTES
TOTAL TIME: 4 TO 5 HOURS**

Without approaching the task via a day-long, low-heat smoking process, we tackle our ribs a little bit more conventionally (and much more simply): We first slow roast our ribs in the oven at a low temperature of 200 degrees for about 3 hours. This allows the acids and seasonings to gently tenderize the meat, while the low heat loosens the meat from the bone so the cooked rib meat will pull away without fuss. We use a covered turkey roasting pan. The cover keeps the moisture inside the roasting pan, which helps the seasoning seep into the meat and tenderizes too. And our pan is long enough to keep the full rack of ribs intact for easier grilling.

INGREDIENTS

2 or 3 cloves garlic, sliced extra thin

1 clove crushed or minced garlic

1 cup honey

1/3 cup dark molasses

1/3 cup dark maple syrup

1 1/2 tablespoons paprika

1 teaspoon sea salt

1 1/2 teaspoons fresh ground pepper

1 tablespoon ancho chili powder (add more if you like your BBQ extra spicy)

2 teaspoons ground cumin

1/2 cup apple cider vinegar (the more you add, the tangier the flavor)

1 1/2 cups organic strained tomatoes

5 or 6 ounces organic tomato paste (no sugar added)

1/4 cup chili sauce

1/4 cup Worcestershire sauce

1 1/2 tablespoons fresh-squeezed lemon juice

5 tablespoons chopped onions

1 teaspoon mustard powder

1/2 pineapple, cubed (if fresh juice collects on your cutting board, add that in too!)

4 to 5 pounds baby back pork ribs

Continued on next page >

< Continued from previous page

1 Preheat the oven to 325 degrees. Meanwhile, mix the BBQ sauce ingredients—all the ingredients except the ribs themselves—in a large sauce pan over low to medium heat allowing the sugars to melt. Line the bottom of the roasting pan with a thick layer of BBQ sauce.

2 Place each rack of ribs into the roasting pan, layering them with a solid basting of the sauce so both sides of each rack of ribs are fully coated. Cover and put the roasting pan in the oven and allow the ribs to cook for $2^{1}/_{2}$ to 3 hours. No need to turn or recoat the ribs during this process.

3 About 15 to 20 minutes before the ribs have finished cooking in your oven, fire up your grill. A gas grill will work just fine, but there's nothing better than wood grilled BBQ ribs so consider your options carefully! Look to achieve a medium heat from your grill.

4 Use long tongs that will allow you to slide the tong the full length of the rack of ribs. This will help prevent the ribs from breaking off as the ribs will be soft and tender from their time in the oven.

5 Basting is perhaps the most important final step in preparing killer ribs. Continually baste the ribs to achieve a beautiful dark brown and black glazed surface. As soon as the flames char an edge of the meat, quickly baste over that area with a fresh coat of sauce and turn the ribs so the opposite side can be lightly and evenly charred by the fire as well. The more layers of sauce, the richer the taste and the more gratifying the dining experience. Don't worry about a little bit of blackening and charring; paint over all the charred areas with a fresh coat of BBQ sauce and the two flavors will wed together.

6 As soon as the ribs reach the level of browning and blackening you desire, remove the ribs from the grill and place them onto a serving tray. Do not place them back into the roasting pan. Bring the ribs directly to the table and allow them to cool to the touch before digging in.

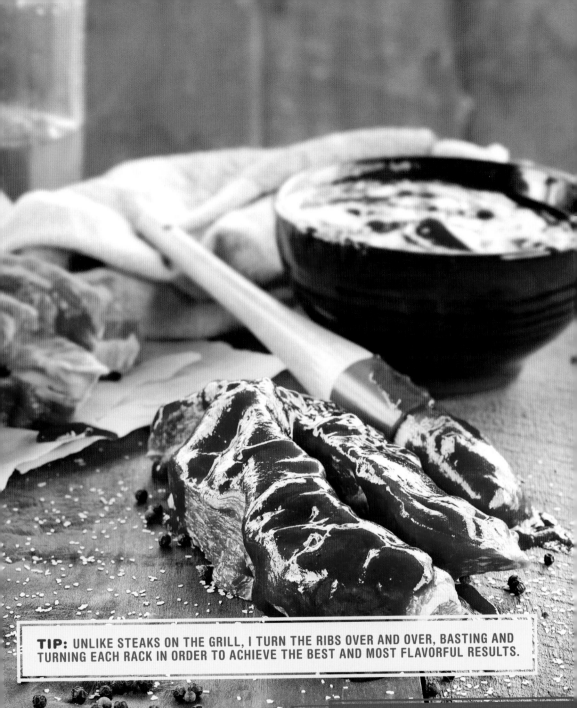

TIP: UNLIKE STEAKS ON THE GRILL, I TURN THE RIBS OVER AND OVER, BASTING AND TURNING EACH RACK IN ORDER TO ACHIEVE THE BEST AND MOST FLAVORFUL RESULTS.

Blueberry Pork Chops

**MAKES 4 TO 6 SERVINGS • ACTIVE TIME: 1 HOUR AND 20 MINUTES
TOTAL TIME: 2 HOURS**

Pork goes so well with sweet fruits, and blueberry is no exception!

INGREDIENTS

- 4 to 5 spare rib pork chops
- Flour for dusting pork chops
- 2 tablespoons clarified butter
- 3 tablespoons of olive oil
- ¾ cup of red wine
- Salt and pepper, to taste
- 2¾ cups of blueberries
- ½ cup of honey

1 Get your grill started, shooting for a temperature of about 375 to 400 degrees. Meanwhile, dust your chops with flour.

2 Melt the clarified butter and olive oil in a saucepan that can withstand the flames of your grill. Add the pork chops and cook over the grill until evenly browned.

3 Add the wine and cook off the alcohol and to reduce the wine so it becomes a nice flavorful stock, and add salt and pepper to taste.

4 Mix the blueberries and the honey in a food blender, one that will allow you to easily spatula off the blueberry honey concoction from the bottom and sides of the blender. A food processor works wonders in this situation as it has a nice wide opening.

5 Coat the pork chops with the blueberry-honey mixture and grill them over the open flame to sear-in the final flavors, about 5 minutes on each side.

6 As the chops have already cooked in the saucepan, they should not need more than a minute or two on each side before being ready to serve. We always try to let our meats and chops stand for about 10 minutes before serving.

Cider-Glazed

MAKES 4 SERVINGS • ACTIVE TIME: 1 HOUR
TOTAL TIME: 4 HOURS AND 30 MINUTES

This is a perfect main dish for a cool fall evening. Butterfly the hens beforehand, as this will allow the breasts to be cooked evenly.

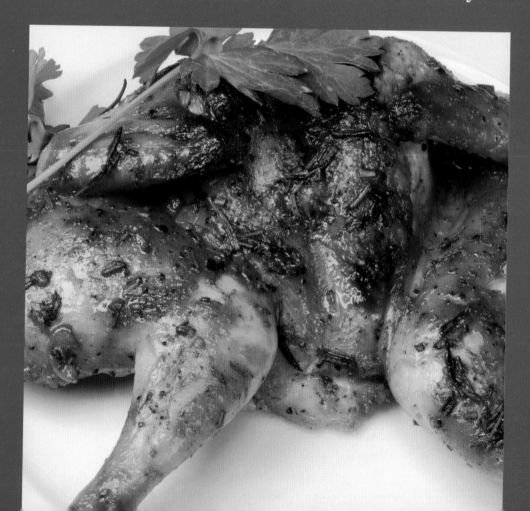

Cornish Hens

1 Season the Cornish hens with coarsely ground black pepper and sea salt. Combine the olive oil, thyme, tarragon, and lemon juice in a small bowl and then place the Cornish hens into the mixture. Let marinate at room temperature for 2 to 4 hours, turning the hens about every 30 minutes so that the marinade coats them evenly.

2 Prepare your gas or charcoal grill to medium-heat and designate two separate heat sections on the grill, one for direct heat and the other for indirect. To do this, simply arrange the coals toward one side of the grill.

3 While waiting for the grill, combine the glaze ingredients in a small saucepan over medium-high heat. Bring the glaze to a boil and reduce to $\frac{1}{4}$ cup, about 10 minutes. Remove from heat and transfer to a small basting bowl.

4 When the grill is ready, at about 400 degrees with the coals lightly covered with ash, brush the glaze over the Cornish hens. Then, place the birds skin-side down over direct heat and cook for 3 minutes. When the skin is a little crispy, flip and move over indirect heat. Cook for about another 25 minutes, basting with the remaining glaze frequently, until the hens are cooked through.

5 Move the Cornish hens from the grill to a large carving board. Let rest for 5 to 10 minutes before serving.

CORNISH HEN INGREDIENTS

Four 1¼-pound Cornish hens, butterflied (see "Chicken Under Brick" recipe, page 310)

Coarsely ground black pepper

Fresh sea salt

¼ cup olive oil

1 sprig thyme, leaves removed

1 sprig tarragon, leaves removed

½ small lemon, juiced

GLAZE INGREDIENTS

1 cup apple cider

1 tablespoon honey

¼ cup clarified butter

Classic Buffalo Wings

Perfect for a Sunday with the boys, this dish never gets old. For this recipe, I decided to add a smoky flavor to the wings by adding a couple cups of pre-soaked hickory or oak woodchips to the coals. This style is optional, though I strongly recommend it.

TOOLS

2 to 3 cups hickory or
oak woodchips

INGREDIENTS

2 pounds chicken wings, split

2 tablespoons clarified butter

3 garlic cloves, minced

¼ teaspoon cayenne

¼ teaspoon paprika

2 teaspoons Tabasco

¼ cup Frank's RedHot®
Cayenne Pepper Sauce

1 head celery, stalks cut into
3-inch pieces

Continued on next page >

< Continued from previous page

1 Place the chicken wings on a roasting pan and put it in the refrigerator. Let rest for at least 2 hours so that the skin on the wings tightens, promoting a crisp wing.

2 One hour before grilling, add the woodchips into a bowl of water and let soak.

3 A half hour before grilling, prepare your gas or charcoal grill to high heat.

4 In a small saucepan, add the clarified butter over medium heat. When hot, add the garlic and cook until golden—about 2 minutes. Next, mix in all of the remaining ingredients (except the celery, of course) and bring to a simmer of medium heat. Simmer for about 3 minutes and then remove from heat and place in a large bowl.

5 Remove the chicken wings from the refrigerator and toss with the buffalo sauce in the large bowl.

6 When the grill is ready, at about 450 degrees with the coals lightly covered with ash, scatter the woodchips over the coals and then place the chicken wings on the grill with a good amount of space between them. Cover the grill and cook for about 2 to 3 minutes on each side, frequently basting each wing with the remaining buffalo sauce. Remove from grill when the skin is crispy.

7 Place on a large serving platter and serve warm alongside celery.

Basil Chicken Breasts with Chile Oil

MAKES 4 SERVINGS • ACTIVE TIME: 20 MINUTES • TOTAL TIME: 6 TO 24 HOURS

While the chicken consists of a soft, basil flavor, the chile oil always comes in with a semi-strong burst of heat. To be safe, serve the chile oil on the side.

CHICKEN INGREDIENTS

2 cups fresh basil leaves

3 scallions, chopped

2 garlic cloves

1 chile pepper of your choice, stemmed and coarsely chopped

¼ to ½ cup olive oil

4 skin-on boneless chicken breasts

Coarsely ground black pepper

Fresh sea salt

CHILE OIL INGREDIENTS

2 chile peppers of your choice

¾ cup olive oil

1 garlic clove, crushed

1 teaspoon ground coriander

Continued on next page >

< Continued from previous page

1 Add chile peppers to a small saucepan over medium-high heat. Lightly toast until the skin is blackened, about 3 to 4 minutes. Remove the chiles and set aside. Next, add $3/4$ cup olive oil to the saucepan and heat. Mix in garlic clove and coriander and cook for 4 to 5 minutes. Then add the chiles and cook for 4 more minutes. Remove and, once cooled, refrigerate overnight.

2 Mix the basil leaves, scallions, garlic, and chile pepper in a large bowl, and then add olive oil. Add the chicken breasts to the marinade and place in the refrigerator. Let soak for at least 4 hours or overnight.

3 Remove the chile oil from the refrigerator and set aside. Also, transfer the chicken from the marinade to a large cutting board and let rest at room temperature for 30 minutes to 1 hour. Leave the marinade near the grill.

4 Prepare your gas or charcoal grill to medium-high heat.

5 When the grill is ready, at about 400 to 450 degrees with the coals lightly covered with ash, place the chicken on the grill and cook for about 7 minutes, frequently basting with the marinade. Flip and grill for another 5 to 6 minutes until finished; they should feel springy if poked with a finger.

6 Remove and let rest for 5 minutes. Serve warm with the chile oil on the side.

TIP: YOU CAN STORE THE CHILE OIL UP TO 4 MONTHS. BUT KEEP IN MIND THAT THE LONGER THE CHILE INFUSES INTO THE OIL, THE HOTTER IT WILL BE!

Chicken Under Brick with Cilantro Oil

MAKES 4 TO 5 SERVINGS • ACTIVE TIME: 1 HOUR • TOTAL TIME: 2 HOURS

This is a classic style of chicken that involves first butterflying the whole chicken, and then cooking it skin-side up with a brick, wrapped in aluminum foil, resting on top. The brick enables the chicken to be cooked through perfectly with charred, crispy skin.

1 To butterfly the chicken, place the chicken skin-side down on a large cutting board. Then, using a strong set of kitchen shears, cut along the backbone and then remove it. Next, flip over the chicken and flatten the breastbone by pressing it down with your palm.

2 Rub the oil on the chicken and then season with the coarsely ground pepper and sea salt.

3 Prepare your gas or charcoal grill. Designate two separate heat sections on the grill, one for direct heat and the other for indirect heat.

4 When the grill is ready, at about 350 to 400 degrees with the coals lightly covered with ash, place the chicken skin-side down over indirect heat. Lay the two bricks across the chicken and grill until the skin is crisp, about 25 to 30 minutes. Next, using tongs or thick oven mitts, remove the bricks from the chicken and set aside. Flip the chicken and lay the bricks on top. Cover the grill and cook for another 20 minutes until the skin is crisp and a meat thermometer, inserted into the thickest part of the thigh, reads 160 degrees.

5 Transfer the chicken to a large carving board.

6 Put the cilantro, garlic, and lime juice into a food processer. Blend into a paste and then slowly add the olive oil until you reach a consistency you prefer.

7 Carve the chicken and lightly drizzle with the cilantro oil.

TOOLS

2 bricks wrapped with aluminum foil

Food processor

CHICKEN INGREDIENTS

A 1¼- to 4-pound whole chicken

2 tablespoons olive oil

2 tablespoons coarsely ground pepper

2 tablespoons fresh sea salt

CILANTRO OIL INGREDIENTS

2 bunches of fresh cilantro, leaves removed

2 garlic cloves, minced

1 small lime, juiced

¼ to ½ cup olive oil

Grilled Meatballs in Marinara Sauce

Who doesn't love homemade meatballs in a traditional marinara sauce?

MEATBALL INGREDIENTS

1 pound ground beef

1 pound ground veal

1 large yellow onion, finely chopped

¼ cup flour

3 garlic cloves, minced

2 large eggs, beaten

¼ cup tablespoons flat-leaf parsley, minced

2 tablespoons basil leaves, minced

1 tablespoon red pepper flakes

Fresh sea salt

MARINARA INGREDIENTS

¼ cup olive oil, plus 2 tablespoons

4 garlic cloves, minced

2 pounds plum tomatoes, crushed by hand

1 sprig oregano

1 sprig rosemary

1 sprig thyme

¼ cup dry white wine

½ cup basil, finely chopped

1 teaspoon coarsely ground black pepper

1 teaspoon fresh sea salt

Continued on next page >

< Continued from previous page

1 In a large bowl, combine the beef, veal, and onion with your hands, and then slowly add in the flour. Let rest for 5 minutes and then add in the rest of the ingredients. Let stand at room temperature for 30 minutes.

2 A half hour before cooking, place a cast-iron skillet on your gas or charcoal grill and prepare the grill to medium-high heat. Leave covered while heating, as it will add a faint smoky flavor to the skillet.

3 Using your hands, firmly form the meat into balls 1½ to 2 inches wide. Place on a plate and set it near the grill.

4 When the grill is ready, about 400 degrees and lightly covered with ash, add 2 tablespoons of olive oil into the skillet. When hot, add the meatballs one by one and sear on all sides for about 8 minutes, or until all sides are browned. Remove from skillet and set aside.

5 Add ¼ cup of olive oil to the skillet, scraping off brown bits from the bottom. When the oil is hot, add the garlic and cook until golden, about 30 seconds to 1 minute—do not let brown. Add the tomatoes, oregano, rosemary, thyme, and the seared meatballs. Simmer for 15 minutes. Add the wine, basil, pepper, and salt and simmer for 20 more minutes, until the meatballs are cooked through.

6 Remove the cast-iron skillet from the grill and spoon the meatballs and sauce into warmed bowls.

VARIATION: If you would like, stir in some grilled shishito peppers to the sauce just before serving as they will add a slightly spicy flavor the sauce.

Lamb Meatballs in Spicy Tomato Sauce

MAKES 4 SERVINGS • ACTIVE TIME: 45 MINUTES
TOTAL TIME: 2 HOURS AND 30 MINUTES

The lamb meatball is very different than that of the beef. The flavor is much more compact in these meatballs, and as such these meatballs will last for several days afterward. They work both as an appetizer and main course, and after the day of grilling, they work perfectly as a mid-day snack.

TOOLS

Cast-iron skillet

LAMB INGREDIENTS

1 medium white onion, finely diced

1 garlic clove, minced

2 whole eggs, whisked

1 teaspoon ground cumin

1 teaspoon dried oregano

½ teaspoon ground cinnamon

2 pounds ground lamb

¼ cup flat-leaf parsley, finely chopped

Coarsely ground black pepper

Fresh sea salt

MARINARA INGREDIENTS

¼ cup olive oil, plus 2 tablespoons

3 garlic cloves, minced

28-ounce can whole tomatoes

1 sprig oregano

1 sprig rosemary

1 sprig thyme

½ teaspoon ground cumin

1 teaspoon red pepper flakes

¼ cup dry white wine

Handful of fresh basil leaves

Coarsely ground black pepper

Fresh sea salt

Continued on next page >

< Continued from previous page

1 In a large bowl, mix together the onion, garlic, whisked eggs, cumin, oregano, and cinnamon. Next, knead the lamb into the bowl with your hands, making sure to toss the ingredients throughout the ground lamb. Let rest for 5 minutes and then add in the parsley, pepper, and salt. Let stand at room temperature for 30 minutes.

2 A half hour before cooking, place a cast-iron skillet on your gas or charcoal grill and prepare the grill to medium-high heat. Leave the cast-iron skillet on the grill while heating so that it develops a faint smoky flavor.

3 Using your hands, firmly form the lamb meat into balls $1^1/_2$ to 2 inches wide. Place on a platter and set it near the grill.

4 When the grill is ready, at about 400 degrees with the coals lightly covered with ash, add 2 tablespoons of olive oil into the skillet. When hot, add the meatballs one by one and sear on all sides for about 8 minutes, or until all sides are browned. Remove from skillet and set aside.

5 Add $^1/_4$ cup of olive oil to the skillet, scraping off brown bits from the bottom. When the oil is hot, add the garlic and cook until golden, about 30 seconds to 1 minute: Do not let brown. Add the tomatoes, oregano, rosemary, thyme, and the seared meatballs. Simmer for 15 minutes. Next, add the ground cumin, red pepper flakes, wine, basil, pepper, and salt and simmer for 20 more minutes, until the meatballs are cooked through.

6 Remove the cast-iron skillet from the grill and spoon the lamb meatballs and sauce into warmed bowls.

Lamb Chops with Parsley-Mint Sauce

**MAKES 4 SERVINGS • ACTIVE TIME: 30 MINUTES
TOTAL TIME: 1 HOUR AND 30 MINUTES**

Mint is one of the more frequently used herbs when used with lamb. And parsley and mint complement each other so well. Be sure to make a little extra of the sauce, as it always seems to go so quickly!

CHOPS INGREDIENTS

2 garlic cloves

2 tablespoons rosemary, finely chopped

2 tablespoons olive oil

4 lamb chops, about 1¼ inches thick

Coarsely ground black pepper

Fresh sea salt

SAUCE INGREDIENTS

1 garlic clove, finely chopped

1 cup flat-leaf parsley, finely chopped

¼ cup mint leaves, finely chopped

2 anchovies, finely chopped (optional)

¼ small lemon, juiced

½ cup olive oil

Coarsely ground black pepper

Fresh sea salt

Continued on next page >

< Continued from previous page

1 In a small bowl, combine the garlic, rosemary, and olive oil. Pour the contents of the bowl onto the lamb chops and then let rest at room temperature for 1 hour.

2 A half hour before grilling, prepare your gas or charcoal grill to medium-high heat.

3 While waiting, in a small bowl, mix together the garlic, parsley, mint, anchovies (optional), and lemon juice. Gradually whisk in the olive oil, and then season with coarsely ground black pepper and fresh sea salt. Transfer to the refrigerator.

4 When the grill is ready, at about 400 to 450 degrees with the coals lightly covered with ash, season one side of the chops with coarsely ground pepper and sea salt. Place the seasoned sides of the chops on the grill at medium heat. Wait 3 minutes until they are slightly charred. A minute before flipping, season the uncooked sides of the chops with the remaining pepper and sea salt. Turn the chops and grill for another 3 minutes for medium-rare or about 4 minutes for medium. The chops should feel slightly firm if poked in the center.

5 Remove the lamb chops from the grill and transfer to a large cutting board. Let stand for 10 minutes, allowing the lamb to properly store its juices and flavor. Serve warm alongside chilled parsley-mint sauce.

Grilled Red Snapper with Chile-Tomato Sauce

MAKES 4 SERVINGS • **ACTIVE TIME: 25 MINUTES** • **TOTAL TIME: 1 HOUR**

Red snapper grills well because of its firm texture and mild flavor, and it is complemented by a little bit of heat as in this chile-tomato sauce.

SNAPPER INGREDIENTS

- 4 red snapper fillets, skin-on and about 1½ to 2 inches thick
- 2 tablespoons olive oil
- 2 teaspoons red pepper flakes (optional)
- Coarsely ground black pepper
- Fresh sea salt

SAUCE INGREDIENTS

- 2 chile peppers of your choice
- 2 tablespoons olive oil
- 1 small shallot, finely chopped
- 2 garlic cloves, minced
- 2 pounds large tomatoes, crushed
- ¼ cup fresh cilantro, finely chopped
- 1 tablespoon flat-leaf parsley, finely chopped
- 2 tablespoons fresh chives, finely chopped
- Coarsely ground black pepper
- Fresh sea salt

Continued on next page >

< Continued from previous page

1 Rub the snapper fillets with olive oil and then season with the red pepper flakes, coarsely ground black pepper, and sea salt. Let stand at room temperature while preparing the grill and the chile-tomato sauce.

2 A half hour before cooking, place a cast-iron skillet on your gas or charcoal grill and prepare to medium heat. Leave the grill covered while heating, as it will add a faint smoky flavor to the skillet.

3 When the grill is ready, at about 400 degrees with the coals lightly covered with ash, add the chile peppers and cook until the chiles are charred and wrinkled. Remove from pan and transfer to a small cutting board. Let cool and then stem the chiles. Finely chop them and set aside.

4 Add the olive oil to the cast-iron skillet. When hot, add the shallot and garlic cloves and cook until the shallot is translucent and the garlic is golden, about 2 minutes. Add the finely chopped chiles into the pan and sear for 1 minute. Mix in the tomatoes and cook until they have broken down. Stir in the cilantro, parsley, and chives and sear for a few more minutes. Season with the pepper and salt and transfer to a bowl. While the sauce is still hot, mash with a fork and cover with aluminum foil.

5 Place the seasoned snapper fillets on the grill directly over the heat source. Cover the grill and cook for about 3 minutes per side. When finished, the fillets should be opaque in the center and should easily tear when pierced with a fork. Transfer to a carving board and peel back the skin. Let rest 5 to 10 minutes, and then serve on beds of chile-tomato sauce.

AT FISH MARKETS ESPECIALLY, THEY FREQUENTLY USE U/10 OR U/15 SCALLOPS. THIS SIMPLY MEANS THAT THERE ARE UNDER 10 OR UNDER 15 SCALLOPS PER POUND; IN OTHER WORDS, THE LOWER THE NUMBER, THE LARGER THE SCALLOP.

Grilled Peach Scallops with Basil-Cilantro Purée

MAKES 4 TO 6 SERVINGS • ACTIVE TIME: 45 MINUTES
TOTAL TIME: 2 HOURS AND 20 MINUTES

Scallops have a very delicate flavor. Although they seem very small, scallops are an extremely filling dish and do not require a large side to accompany them, maybe just a small salad.

SCALLOP INGREDIENTS

4 large, ripe peaches, cut into ¼-inch cubes

2 tablespoons olive oil

15 u/10 or u/15 diver scallops

Lime wedge (for juicing)

Coarsely ground black pepper

Fresh sea salt

BASIL-CILANTRO PURÉE

½ cup fresh cilantro leaves

½ cup fresh basil leaves

2 tablespoons fresh flat-leaf parsley leaves

2 garlic cloves, minced

2 tablespoons jalapeño, finely chopped

½ small lime, juiced

¼ cup olive oil

Coarsely ground black pepper

Fresh sea salt

Continued on next page >

< Continued from previous page

1 In a large bowl, combine the cubed peaches and olive oil. Let rest for about 30 minutes, until the juices from the peaches blanket the bottom of the bowl.

2 Season the diver scallops with a little lemon juice, coarsely ground black pepper, and sea salt and then add them into the peach mixture, making sure that most of them are covered. Let the scallops marinate in the refrigerator for 1 to $1\frac{1}{2}$ hours.

3 Prepare your gas or charcoal grill for medium heat, designating 2 sections: one for direct heat and the other for indirect. To do so, simply pile the coals on one side of the grill.

4 While waiting for the grill, combine the cilantro, basil, parsley, garlic, and jalepeño in a small food processor. Blend into a thick paste, and then gradually add in the lime juice and olive oil until you reach a desired consistency. Season with ground pepper and sea salt, then remove from food processor and set aside.

5 When the grill is ready, at about 400 degrees with the coals lightly covered with ash, place the diver scallops over indirect heat. Cover the grill and cook for about 5 to 6 minutes, flipping once, until the scallops are firm and lightly charred. To check for doneness, insert a fork into the center and if it comes out cold, cook for another minute or so; if it comes out warm, remove the scallops from the grill.

6 Let the diver scallops rest on a carving board for 5 minutes, then plate. Drizzle the basil-cilantro purée over the scallops and to the side. Serve warm.

VARIATION: For more heat, use 2 tablespoons habanero instead of the jalepeño.

Grill-Seared Lemon Haddock

MAKES 4 To 5 SERVINGS • ACTIVE TIME: 20 MINUTES • TOTAL TIME: 40 MINUTES

A properly cooked haddock will be flakey with soft flavors. As such, the nutty flavor in the basil-walnut pesto works perfectly alongside the haddock.

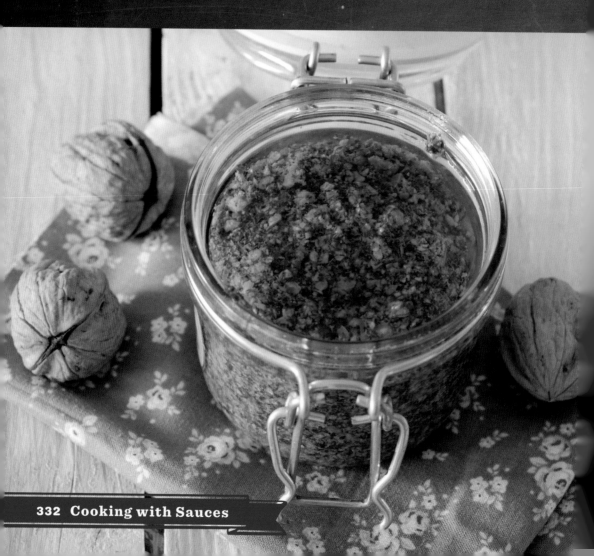

with Basil-Walnut Pesto

1 Place the haddock fillets to a small baking pan and then add the olive oil. Season the fillets with coarsely ground black pepper and sea salt, then with freshly squeezed lemon juice. Let rest at room temperature while preparing the grill.

2 A half hour before cooking, place a cast-iron skillet on your gas or charcoal grill and prepare to medium heat. Leave the grill covered while heating, as it will add a faint smoky flavor to the skillet.

3 While the grill heats, purée the walnuts, basil, cilantro, and garlic cloves in a small food processor. When the mixture is a thick paste, slowly blend in the olive oil until you reach a consistency you like. Remove from food processor, season with black pepper and salt, and set aside.

4 When the grill is ready, at about 400 to 500 degrees with the coals lightly covered with ash, add the fillets to the skillet and sear for about 5 minutes. When the fillets have browned, turn and cook for 1 to 2 more minutes, until the fish is opaque through the center.

5 Serve the haddock with the basil-walnut pesto.

HADDOCK INGREDIENTS

1½ pound Alaskan haddock fillets

¼ cup olive oil

Coarsely ground black pepper

Fresh sea salt

1 lemon, halved

PESTO INGREDIENTS

½ cup walnuts

1 bunch fresh basil leaves

1 tablespoon fresh cilantro leaves

2 garlic cloves

½ cup olive oil

Coarsely ground black pepper

Fresh sea salt

Seared Tuna Steaks with Dill Aioli

MAKES 4 SERVINGS • ACTIVE TIME: 25 MINUTES • TOTAL TIME: 50 MINUTES

Seared tuna steaks are always great on a warm summer evening. When serving these steaks, you have the option of serving chilled or right off the grill. The dill aioli is perfect when served slightly chilled.

TUNA STEAKS INGREDIENTS

4 fresh tuna steaks, about 2 inches thick

2 tablespoon olive oil, plus a little extra for the grill

Coarsely ground black pepper

Fresh sea salt

DILL AIOLI INGREDIENTS

10 sprigs dill, finely chopped

10 sprigs parsley, finely chopped

¼ small lemon, juiced

1 garlic clove, minced

¾ cup olive oil

Fresh sea salt

Continued on next page >

< Continued from previous page

1 Rub the tuna steaks with a little olive oil and then season with pepper and salt. Let rest at room temperature while you prepare the grill and dill aioli.

2 Prepare your gas or charcoal grill to high heat.

3 While waiting for the grill, combine the dill, parsley, lemon juice, and garlic into a small bowl and whisk together. While whisking, slowly incorporate the olive oil and then season with fresh sea salt. Set aside or chill in the refrigerator. (If you want a lighter aioli, combine the initial ingredients in a blender and then slowly add the olive oil.)

4 When the grill is ready, at about 450 to 500 degrees with the coals lightly covered with ash, brush the grate with a little olive oil. Tuna steaks should always be cooked between rare and medium-rare; anything over will be tough and dry. To accomplish a perfect searing, place the tuna steaks directly over the hot part of the coals and sear for about 2 minutes per side. The tuna should be raw in the middle (cook $2\frac{1}{2}$ to 3 minutes per side for medium-rare).

5 Transfer the tuna steaks to a large carving board and let rest for 5 to 10 minutes. Slice against the grain and then serve with the dill aioli to the side.

Bastes, Butters, and Glazes

Perhaps no barbecue dinner is complete without bastes, butters, or glazes. In the original version of *Rubs*, I didn't give bastes, butters, and glazes the attention they deserve. Bastes and glazes essentially serve as a marinade to use during the grilling process. The key to a successful baste or glaze is to generously apply them to your desired meat while grilling. The more you apply, the better: a strong baste will add a nice level of moisture to your meat, while a glaze will supply a crisp, glossy layer on the outside. Butters are easy, though crucial: prepare them ahead of time, and then serve 1 tablespoon of your butter alongside each serving.

The All-American BBQ Mop

MAKES 6 SERVINGS • ACTIVE TIME: 15 MINUTES
TOTAL TIME: 1 HOUR AND 15 MINUTES

WORKS BEST WITH:	☑ RED MEAT	☑ PORK	☑ POULTRY	☐ SEAFOOD
FLAVOR:	☐ SPICY	☑ SWEET	☑ TANGY	☑ SAVORY	☑ SALTY
CONSISTENCY:	☐ COARSE	☑ COATING	☐ POURING

In a bowl, combine all of the ingredients and let rest for 1 hour before basting.

INGREDIENTS

½ cup water

½ cup apple cider vinegar

3 tablespoons olive oil

3 tablespoons Dijon mustard

1 tablespoon ground black pepper

1 tablespoon sea salt

2 garlic cloves, chopped

2 teaspoons thyme, minced

Grilled Chicken Basting Sauce

MAKES 4 SERVINGS • ACTIVE TIME: 20 MINUTES
TOTAL TIME: 1 HOUR AND 20 MINUTES

WORKS BEST WITH:	☐ RED MEAT	☑ PORK	☑ POULTRY	☐ SEAFOOD
FLAVOR:	☐ SPICY	☐ SWEET	☐ TANGY	☑ SAVORY ☐ SALTY
CONSISTENCY:	☐ COARSE	☑ COATING	☐ POURING	

INGREDIENTS

¼ cup butter, melted

1 garlic clove, minced

1 teaspoon ground
black pepper

1 teaspoon sea salt

1 teaspoon
rosemary, minced

1 teaspoon thyme, minced

In a bowl, combine all of the ingredients and let rest for 1 hour before basting.

North Carolina Baste

MAKES 8 SERVINGS • ACTIVE TIME: 5 MINUTES
TOTAL TIME: 1 HOUR AND 5 MINUTES

WORKS BEST WITH:	☑ RED MEAT	☑ PORK	☑ POULTRY	☐ SEAFOOD
FLAVOR:	☐ SPICY	☐ SWEET	☑ TANGY	☑ SAVORY	☐ SALTY
CONSISTENCY:	☐ COARSE	☑ COATING	☑ POURING

In a bowl, combine all of the ingredients and let rest for 1 hour before basting.

INGREDIENTS

2 cups apple cider vinegar

2 tablespoons dark brown sugar

1 tablespoon olive oil

2 teaspoons Worcestershire sauce

2 teaspoons red chili flakes

1 teaspoon paprika

1 teaspoon ground black pepper

1 teaspoon sea salt

Honey-Soy Seafood Baste

MAKES 4 SERVINGS • ACTIVE TIME: 10 MINUTES

TOTAL TIME: 1 HOUR AND 10 MINUTES

WORKS BEST WITH: ☐ RED MEAT ☐ PORK ☑ POULTRY ☑ SEAFOOD

FLAVOR: ☐ SPICY ☐ SWEET ☑ TANGY ☐ SAVORY ☑ SALTY

CONSISTENCY: ☐ COARSE ☑ COATING ☐ POURING

INGREDIENTS

3 tablespoons
Dijon mustard

3 tablespoons soy sauce

3 tablespoons honey

2 garlic cloves, minced

¼ cup olive oil

1 teaspoon sesame seeds

In a bowl, combine all of the ingredients and let rest for 1 hour before basting.

Tabasco Butter Baste

MAKES 8 SERVINGS • **ACTIVE TIME: 5 MINUTES** • **TOTAL TIME: 5 MINUTES**

WORKS BEST WITH:	☐ RED MEAT	☐ PORK	☑ POULTRY	☑ SEAFOOD
FLAVOR:	☑ SPICY	☐ SWEET	☑ TANGY	☐ SAVORY	☑ SALTY
CONSISTENCY:	☐ COARSE	☑ COATING	☐ POURING	

In a bowl, whisk together all of the ingredients and baste immediately.

INGREDIENTS

1 stick unsalted butter, melted

3 teaspoons lemon juice

¼ teaspoon Tabasco sauce

¼ teaspoon parsley, minced

Garlic and Chive Butter

WORKS BEST WITH:	☐ RED MEAT	☑ PORK	☑ POULTRY	☑ SEAFOOD
FLAVOR:	☐ SPICY	☐ SWEET	☐ TANGY	☑ SAVORY ☐ SALTY
CONSISTENCY:	☑ COARSE	☐ COATING	☐ POURING	

INGREDIENTS

1 stick unsalted
butter, softened

2 garlic cloves, minced

1 tablespoon
chives, minced

½ teaspoon kosher salt

1 Place all ingredients into a bowl and, using a fork, whisk until thoroughly combined.

2 Reduce the heat to low, and cook for about 1 hour, stirring occasionally, until the sauce has thickened and reduced by half.

3 Cover the bowl with aluminum foil and refrigerate for at least 2 hours before serving.

Herbed Steak Butter

MAKES 8 SERVINGS • **ACTIVE TIME: 20 MINUTES**

TOTAL TIME: 2 HOURS AND 20 MINUTES

WORKS BEST WITH: ☑ RED MEAT ☑ PORK ☐ POULTRY ☐ SEAFOOD

FLAVOR: ☐ SPICY ☐ SWEET ☐ TANGY ☑ SAVORY ☐ SALTY

CONSISTENCY: ☑ COARSE ☐ COATING ☐ POURING

1 Place all ingredients into a bowl and, using a fork, whisk until thoroughly combined.

2 Cover the bowl with aluminum foil and refrigerate for at least 2 hours before serving.

INGREDIENTS

1 stick unsalted butter, softened

½ teaspoon rosemary, minced

½ teaspoon tarragon, minced

½ teaspoon chives, minced

½ teaspoon thyme, minced

Wasabi Butter

MAKES 8 SERVINGS • ACTIVE TIME: 5 MINUTES

TOTAL TIME: 2 HOURS AND 5 MINUTES

WORKS BEST WITH:	☐ RED MEAT	☐ PORK	☐ POULTRY	☑ SEAFOOD
FLAVOR:	☑ SPICY	☐ SWEET	☑ TANGY	☐ SAVORY ☐ SALTY
CONSISTENCY:	☑ COARSE	☐ COATING	☐ POURING	

INGREDIENTS

1 stick unsalted butter, softened

1 teaspoon prepared wasabi

½ teaspoon kosher salt

¼ teaspoon soy sauce

1 Place all ingredients into a bowl and, using a fork, whisk until thoroughly combined.

2 Cover the bowl with aluminum foil and refrigerate for at least 2 hours before serving.

Lemon Butter

WORKS BEST WITH:	☑ RED MEAT	☑ PORK	☑ POULTRY	☑ SEAFOOD
FLAVOR:	☐ SPICY	☐ SWEET	☑ TANGY	☑ SAVORY ☐ SALTY
CONSISTENCY:	☑ COARSE	☐ COATING	☐ POURING	

1 Place all ingredients into a bowl and, using a fork, whisk until thoroughly combined.

2 Cover the bowl with aluminum foil and refrigerate for at least 2 hours before serving.

INGREDIENTS

1 stick unsalted butter, softened

1 teaspoon lemon zest

1 teaspoon lemon juice

½ teaspoon kosher salt

½ teaspoon rosemary, minced

Chili Lime Butter

MAKES 8 SERVINGS • **ACTIVE TIME: 5 MINUTES**

TOTAL TIME: 2 HOURS AND 5 MINUTES

WORKS BEST WITH: ☑ RED MEAT ☑ PORK ☑ POULTRY ☑ SEAFOOD

FLAVOR: ☑ SPICY ☐ SWEET ☐ TANGY ☑ SAVORY ☐ SALTY

CONSISTENCY: ☑ COARSE ☐ COATING ☐ POURING

INGREDIENTS

1 stick unsalted butter, softened

1 tablespoon lime zest

2 teaspoons chili powder

1 teaspoon lime juice

½ teaspoon kosher salt

1 Place all ingredients into a bowl and, using a fork, whisk until thoroughly combined.

2 Cover the bowl with aluminum foil and refrigerate for at least 2 hours before serving.

Sticky BBQ Glaze

MAKES 6 SERVINGS	•	ACTIVE TIME: 5 MINUTES	•	TOTAL TIME: 5 MINUTES

WORKS BEST WITH:	☑ RED MEAT	☑ PORK	☑ POULTRY	☐ SEAFOOD
FLAVOR:	☑ SPICY	☑ SWEET	☑ TANGY	☑ SAVORY	☐ SALTY
CONSISTENCY:	☐ COARSE	☑ COATING	☐ POURING

Place all ingredients into a bowl and, using a fork, whisk until thoroughly combined.

INGREDIENTS

1½ cups light brown sugar

3 tablespoons apple cider vinegar

3 tablespoons water

1 teaspoon red chili flakes

1 teaspoon Dijon mustard

1 teaspoon ground black pepper

1 teaspoon sea salt

Apple Glaze

WORKS BEST WITH:	☐ RED MEAT	☑ PORK	☑ POULTRY	☐ SEAFOOD
FLAVOR:	☐ SPICY	☑ SWEET	☐ TANGY	☑ SAVORY	☐ SALTY
CONSISTENCY:	☐ COARSE	☑ COATING	☐ POURING

1 Heat olive oil in a saucepan over medium heat. Add garlic, and cook until golden, about 2 minutes.

2 Add the apple cider, Dijon mustard, rosemary, black pepper, and sea salt to the saucepan. Cook until the sauce has reduced by half, about 6 to 8 minutes. Season to taste with additional pepper and salt.

3 Remove from heat, let rest for 10 minutes, and then apply to meat.

INGREDIENTS

2 tablespoons olive oil

2 garlic cloves, minced

2 cups apple cider

1 teaspoon Dijon mustard

1 teaspoon rosemary, minced

1 teaspoon ground black pepper

2 teaspoons sea salt

Bourbon and Brown Sugar Glaze

MAKES 6 SERVINGS • ACTIVE TIME: 10 MINUTES • TOTAL TIME: 40 MINUTES

WORKS BEST WITH: ☐ RED MEAT ☑ PORK ☑ POULTRY ☐ SEAFOOD

FLAVOR: ☐ SPICY ☑ SWEET ☐ TANGY ☑ SAVORY ☐ SALTY

CONSISTENCY: ☐ COARSE ☑ COATING ☐ POURING

1 Place a saucepan over medium heat. Add butter and cook until melted.

2 Next, add bourbon, brown sugar, apple cider vinegar, and Dijon mustard to the saucepan. Bring to a simmer, cover the pan, and cook until the mixture has reduced by a third, about 6 minutes.

3 Remove from heat and let settle to room temperature. Apply to meat before and during cooking process.

INGREDIENTS

4 tablespoons butter

½ cup bourbon

½ cup brown sugar

¼ cup apple cider vinegar

1 teaspoon Dijon mustard

1 teaspoon ground black pepper

1 teaspoon sea salt

Sweet Maple BBQ Glaze

MAKES 6 SERVINGS • **ACTIVE TIME: 15 MINUTES** • **TOTAL TIME: 1 HOUR**

WORKS BEST WITH:	☑ RED MEAT	☑ PORK	☑ POULTRY	☐ SEAFOOD
FLAVOR:	☐ SPICY	☑ SWEET	☐ TANGY	☑ SAVORY	☐ SALTY
CONSISTENCY:	☐ COARSE	☑ COATING	☐ POURING	

INGREDIENTS

1 tablespoon olive oil

2 garlic cloves, minced

¾ cup ketchup

1 cup apple cider

¼ cup maple syrup

2 tablespoons apple cider vinegar

1 teaspoon paprika

1 teaspoon Worcestershire sauce

1 teaspoon ground black pepper

1 teaspoon sea salt

1 Heat the olive oil in a saucepan over medium heat. Add the minced garlic cloves, and cook until golden, about 2 minutes.

2 Add the ketchup, apple cider, maple syrup, apple cider vinegar, paprika, and Worcestershire sauce to the saucepan. Bring to a simmer and let cook for about 10 to 15 minutes, until the sauce has reduced by half. Season to taste with ground pepper and sea salt.

3 Remove the glaze from saucepan and let settle to room temperature. Apply to meat before and during the cooking process.

Cooking with Bastes, Butters, and Glazes

Memphis Ribs with All-American BBQ Mop

MAKES 6 TO 8 SERVINGS • **ACTIVE TIME: 1 HOUR** • **TOTAL TIME: 4 HOURS**

1 Preheat your gas or charcoal grill to medium-high. If you are using a charcoal grill, place the coals on one side to differentiate the heat.

2 In a small bowl, combine paprika, kosher salt, and black pepper. Using your hands, generously apply the rub mixture to the baby back ribs, thoroughly kneading so that the rub is secured to the ribs.

3 Place your All-American BBQ Mop alongside the grill so you can baste your baby back ribs while grilling.

4 When the grill is ready and the coals have developed a nice layer of gray ash, place the ribs on the grill (above the coals if using a charcoal grill) and cook for 20 to 25 minutes. Baste the ribs with the All-American BBQ Mop after placing the ribs to the grill, and turn the ribs every 5 minutes or so, making sure to baste when you do so.

5 Check the ribs after 20 to 25 minutes to make sure the meat is cooked (there should be no sign of pink in the meat). Remove and serve immediately.

INGREDIENTS

2 tablespoons paprika

2 tablespoons kosher salt

2 tablespoons coarsely ground black pepper

3 to 4 pounds pork baby back ribs

3 cups All-American BBQ Mop (see page 345)

Grilled Chicken Breasts

MAKES 4 TO 6 SERVINGS • ACTIVE TIME: 20 MINUTES • TOTAL TIME: 25 MINUTES

1 Preheat your gas or charcoal grill to medium-high. If you are using a charcoal grill, place the coals on one side of the grill to differentiate the heat.

2 Season your chicken breasts with sea salt and black pepper. While waiting for the grill to heat up, prepare the Grilled Chicken Basting Sauce and place it alongside the grill.

3 When your grill is hot (roughly 400 degrees and the coals are covered in a gray ash), place your chicken breasts directly over the heat, skin down. Cook for 15 minutes, basting every 5 minutes. After 15 minutes, turn the breasts over and cook for another 10 to 15 minutes, until the skin is browned.

4 Remove from heat, garnish with fresh parsley, and serve immediately.

INGREDIENTS

4 chicken breasts, bone-in and skin-on

2 tablespoons sea salt

2 tablespoons coarsely ground black pepper

3 cups Grilled Chicken Basting Sauce (see page 346)

2 tablespoons fresh parsley, chopped (optional)

Grilled Salmon Fillets using Honey-Soy Seafood Baste

1 In a deep baking dish, season both sides of the salmon fillets with sea salt and black pepper. Next, add 1 cup of the Honey-Soy Seafood Baste to the dish and let marinate for roughly 1 hour in the refrigerator.

2 Preheat your gas or charcoal grill to medium-high. If you are using a charcoal grill, place the coals on one side of the grill to differentiate the heat.

3 When the grill is hot and the salmon fillets have marinated for at least 1 hour, place the fillets skin-down on the grill. Grill the salmon fillets, basting every 3 minutes, for about 13 to 15 minutes, until the fillets are juicy and the meat is flakey.

4 Carefully remove the salmon fillets from the grill, and serve immediately with lemon wedges.

INGREDIENTS

1 large salmon fillet, cut into 6 rectangular slices

2 tablespoons sea salt

2 tablespoons coarsely ground black pepper

3 cups Honey-Soy Seafood Baste (see page 350)

6 small lemon wedges

Skewered Shrimp with Tabasco Butter Baste

MAKES 4 TO 6 SERVINGS • ACTIVE TIME: 10 MINUTES • TOTAL TIME: 25 MINUTES

1 Preheat your gas or charcoal grill to medium-high. If you are using a charcoal grill, place the coals on one side of the grill to differentiate the heat.

2 In a small bowl, toss the shrimp with black pepper and sea salt. Add ¼ cup of the melted Tabasco Butter Baste to the bowl, and combine thoroughly. Skewer the shrimp, leaving about ½ inch between each shrimp.

3 When the grill is hot, place the shrimp skewers over direct heat and cook for 2 to 3 minutes per side, basting constantly. Remove the shrimp from the grill and serve immediately.

TOOLS

6 to 10 bamboo skewers, soaked in water

INGREDIENTS

2 pounds large raw shrimp, deveined

2 tablespoons coarsely ground black pepper

2 tablespoons sea salt

½ cup Tabasco Butter Baste (see page 353)

Flank Steak with Garlic-Chive Butter

MAKES 4 SERVINGS • ACTIVE TIME: 25 MINUTES • TOTAL TIME: 1 HOUR 15 MINUTES

1 Remove the steak from the refrigerator and rub with a mixture of olive oil, rosemary, and thyme. Let rest at room temperature for 1 hour.

2 A half-hour before cooking, preheat your gas or charcoal grill to medium-high.

3 When the grill is ready, about 400 to 450 degrees with the coals lightly covered with ash, season one side of the steak with half of the coarsely ground pepper and sea salt. Place the seasoned side of the steak on the grill and cook for 4 to 5 minutes, seasoning the uncooked side of the steak while waiting. When the steak seems charred, gently flip and cook for 4 to 5 more minutes for medium-rare and 6 more minutes for medium. The steak should feel slightly firm when poked in the center.

4 Remove the steak from the grill and transfer to a large cutting board. Let stand for 6 to 8 minutes. Slice the steak diagonally into long, thin slices, and place a tablespoon of the Garlic and Chive Butter alongside each serving.

INGREDIENTS

1 flank steak, about 1 to 1½ pounds

2 tablespoons olive oil

2 sprigs of rosemary, leaves removed

2 sprigs of thyme, leaves removed

2 tablespoons coarsely ground black pepper

2 tablespoons sea salt

½ cup Garlic & Chive Butter (see page 354)

Grilled Tuna Steaks with Wasabi Butter

1 Rub the tuna steaks with a little olive oil and then season with pepper and salt. Let rest at room temperature while you prepare the grill.

2 Preheat your gas or charcoal grill to high.

3 When the grill is ready, at about 450 to 500 degrees with the coals lightly covered with ash, brush the grate with a little olive oil. Tuna steaks should always be cooked between rare and medium-rare; anything more will make them tough and dry. To accomplish a perfect sear, place the tuna steaks directly over the hot part of the coals and sear for about 2 minutes per side. The tuna should be raw in the middle (cook 2½ to 3 minutes per side for medium-rare).

4 Transfer the tuna steaks to a large carving board and let rest for 5 to 10 minutes. Slice against the grain and then serve each tuna steak with 1 tablespoon of Wasabi Butter.

INGREDIENTS

4 fresh tuna steaks, about
2 inches thick

2 tablespoons olive oil,
plus a little extra
for the grill

2 tablespoons coarsely
ground black pepper

2 tablespoons sea salt

½ cup Wasabi Butter
(see page 358)

Grilled Lime Mahi-Mahi with Chili Lime Butter

MAKES 4 SERVINGS • ACTIVE TIME: 25 MINUTES

TOTAL TIME: 1 HOUR TO 2 HOURS, DEPENDING ON MARINATING TIME

1 In a medium roasting pan, combine the olive oil, lime juice, garlic, red pepper flakes, and cayenne pepper and mix thoroughly. Place the mahi-mahi fillets into the marinade and let stand at room temperature for 1 to 2 hours, flipping once

2 Preheat your gas or charcoal grill to high.

3 Remove the mahi-mahi fillets from the marinade and place directly over the heat. Cover the grill and cook for about 4 to 5 minutes per side, until the fillets are flakey and moist when touched with a fork.

4 Remove the fillets from the grill and serve immediately. Serve each fillet alongside 1 tablespoon of Chili Lime Butter.

INGREDIENTS

½ cup olive oil

½ small lime, juiced

1 garlic clove, minced

1 teaspoon red pepper flakes

½ teaspoon cayenne pepper

4 mahi-mahi fillets

2 tablespoons coarsely ground black pepper

2 tablespoons sea salt

½ cup Chili Lime Butter (see page 362)

Grilled Whole Striped Bass with Lemon Butter

MAKES 4 SERVINGS • ACTIVE TIME: 25 MINUTES • TOTAL TIME: 1 HOUR 15 MINUTES

1 Squeeze the orange half over the whole striped bass. Next, season with the rosemary leaves, coarsely ground black pepper, and sea salt. Cover with aluminum foil and let rest at room temperature for about 1 hour.

2 Preheat your gas or charcoal grill to medium-high.

3 When the grill is ready, at about 450 to 500 degrees with the coals lightly covered with ash, place the whole striped bass on the grill for about 6 to 7 minutes, then flip. Cook the fish for another 6 to 7 minutes, until the fish is juicy and opaque in the middle.

4 Remove the striped bass from the grill and transfer to a large cutting board. Cover and let rest for 5 to 10 minutes before serving. Serve each serving with 1 tablespoon of lemon butter on the side.

INGREDIENTS

½ large orange

2 whole striped bass, about 2 pounds each, gutted, cleaned, fins removed

2 sprigs rosemary, leaves removed

2 tablespoons coarsely ground black pepper

2 tablespoons fresh sea salt

½ cup Lemon Butter (see page 361)

Baby Back Pork Ribs with Bourbon and Brown Sugar Glaze

MAKES 4 TO 6 SERVINGS • ACTIVE TIME: 25 MINUTES • TOTAL TIME: 45 MINUTES

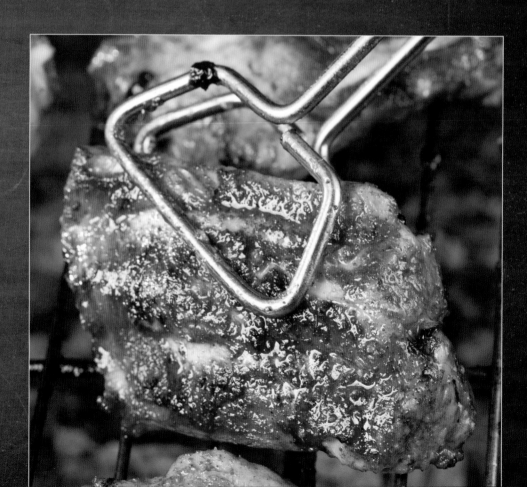

1 Preheat your gas or charcoal grill to medium-high. If you are using a charcoal grill, place the coals on one side of the grill to differentiate the heat.

2 In a medium roasting dish, combine the kosher salt and black pepper. Using your hands, generously apply the mixture to the baby back ribs, thoroughly kneading so that the rub is secured to the ribs. Add 1 cup of the Bourbon and Brown Sugar Glaze to the roasting dish, and coat the ribs thoroughly.

3 Place your remaining 2 cups of Bourbon and Brown Sugar Glaze alongside the grill so that you can baste your baby back ribs while grilling.

4 When the grill is ready and the coals have developed a nice layer of gray ash, place the ribs over the grill (above the coals if using a charcoal grill) and cook for 20 to 25 minutes. Baste the ribs with the Bourbon and Brown Sugar Glaze after applying to the grill, and turn the ribs every 5 minutes or so, making sure to baste when you do. A glossy coat should form on the outside of the ribs.

5 Check the ribs after 20 to 25 minutes to make sure the meat is cooked (there should be no sign of pink in the meat). Remove and serve immediately.

INGREDIENTS

2 tablespoons kosher salt

2 tablespoons coarsely ground black pepper

3 to 4 pounds pork baby back ribs

3 cups Bourbon and Brown Sugar Glaze (see page 369)

Chicken Under Brick with Apple Glaze

MAKES 4 TO 6 SERVINGS • ACTIVE TIME: 40 MINUTES
TOTAL TIME: 1 HOUR AND 10 MINUTES

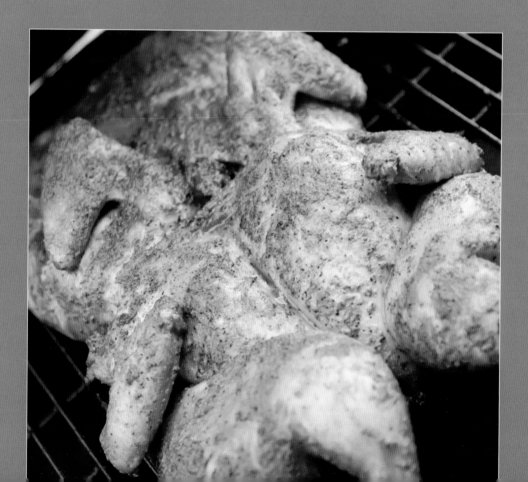

1 To butterfly the chicken, place it skin-side down on a large cutting board. Then, using a strong set of kitchen shears, cut along the backbone and then remove it. Flip the chicken over and flatten the breastbone by pressing down with your palm.

2 Rub the oil on the chicken and then season with the coarsely ground pepper and sea salt. Using your hands, apply 1 cup of the Apple Glaze to the chicken. Let the chicken stand at room temperature for 30 minutes. .

3 Preheat your gas or charcoal grill. When cooking this dish, you want to designate two separate heat sections on the grill, one for direct heat and the other for indirect heat. To do this, simply arrange the coals on one side of the grill.

4 When the grill is ready, at about 350 to 400 degrees with the coals lightly covered with ash, place the chicken skin-side down over indirect heat. Lay the two bricks across the chicken and grill until the skin is crisp, about 25 to 30 minutes. Baste once or twice with the remaining 2 cups of Apple Glaze. Next, using tongs or thick oven mitts, remove the bricks and set aside. Flip the chicken and lay the bricks on top. Cover the grill and cook for another 20 minutes, basting once or twice, until the skin is crisp and a meat thermometer, inserted into the thickest part of the thigh, reads 160 degrees.

5 Transfer the chicken to a large cutting board and let rest for 10 to 15 minutes before serving.

TOOLS

2 bricks wrapped in aluminum foil

INGREDIENTS

4- to 5-pound whole chicken

2 tablespoons olive oil

2 tablespoons coarsely ground pepper

2 tablespoons fresh sea salt

3 cups Apple Glaze (see page 366)

Index